D1104424

CAROLINE M. HEWINS
HER BOOK

Containing

A MID-CENTURY CHILD AND HER BOOKS

BY CAROLINE M. HEWINS

CAROLINE M. HEWINS AND BOOKS FOR CHILDREN

BY JENNIE D. LINDQUIST

THE HORN BOOK, INC. · BOSTON · 1954

PREFACE

I T was a festival day for me when I visited the Public Library in Hartford in May, 1916, and sat in Miss Hewins' office beside her collection of children's books gathered over a lifetime. This was the day when she promised to write an introduction to our first *Recommended Purchase List of Books for Boys and Girls*. This introduction was devoted to " juvenile libraries " of the past and specifically to the first bookshop for children established by John Newbery in London of the mid-1700s. We prized this introduction and reprinted it in *Realms of Gold*. There was also transmitted to me that day a wonderful dynamic of encouragement, for Miss Hewins had faith as well as interest in the new Bookshop for Boys and Girls. From the time of its opening until her death she was a frequent visitor.

Miss Hewins' own recollections of her childhood reading in *A Mid-Century Child* make a wonderfully complete and far-reaching record, and it seemed appropriate to re-issue it along with Miss Lindquist's Hewins Lecture so that young librarians might have a well-rounded impression of an unusual woman who found her way into library work for children when the route was uncharted and far more solitary than it is today.

Because Frederic G. Melcher felt that Miss Hewins deserved a permanent place of honor in the children's library field, on October 19, 1946, at the 40th anniversary meeting of the New England Round Table of Children's Librarians, he brought the Hewins Lecture into being, recommending that the Round

v

Table select each year a person to write a paper on a subject of importance in the field of children's books. The lecturer was to be a resident of New England and connected with library work for children or young people.

Jennie D. Lindquist, now editor of *The Horn Book Magazine*, was the first person to be awarded the Hewins Scholarship and it seems particularly fitting that her Lecture on Miss Hewins be included in this volume.

The first Hewins Lecture was given by Alice M. Jordan at the fall meeting of the Round Table and the New England Library Association in 1947, her subject being the reading of New England children in the 1870s. This Lecture, entitled "From Rollo to Tom Sawyer and Other Papers," was published in book form by The Horn Book, Inc., in 1948. The complete list of Hewins Lectures, their titles and authors will be found on page ix of this book.

BERTHA MAHONY MILLER

CONTENTS

vii

THE CAROLINE M. HEWINS LECTURES

1947-1954

The Hewins Lectures have been published regularly, in whole or in part, in *The Horn Book Magazine*, and Miss Jordan's lecture is available in book form (*From Rollo to Tom Sawyer and Other Papers*, Horn Book, Inc., 1948).

ILLUSTRATIONS

A MID-CENTURY CHILD
AND HER BOOKS

By Caroline M. Hewins

From " Peter Parley's Winter Evening Tales "

INTRODUCTION

"Ever since the Winter's evening when I made my first acquaintance with that delightful place," writes Anne Thackeray Ritchie in her introduction to CRANFORD, " it has seemed to me something of a visionary country home which I have visited all my life long (in spirit) for refreshment and change of scene. I have been there in good company. ' Thank you for your letter,' Charlotte Brontë writes to Mrs. Gaskell. ' It was as pleasant as a quiet chat, as welcome as spring showers, as reviving as a friend's visit; in short, it was very like a page of CRANFORD'."

The copy of CRANFORD from which I have quoted, with its delicately tinted drawings by Hugh Thomson, was a Christmas gift from Caroline Hewins in one of the early years of a friendship singularly rich in intimate associations with children and in the discovery of new and old books that children like. There is a likeness between Lady Ritchie's picture of Cranford and my own feeling for Miss Hewins's office in the Hartford Public Library. No " lofty pleasure-dome in Xanadu " did she rear for her dear friends, the books of her choice, but with the touch of a born magician she transformed an ordinary library room into a spacious hall of enchantment worthy of the mid-century child who fell in love with THE ALHAMBRA at the age of ten. At home anywhere in the world, in this enchanting room one finds

Caroline Hewins nearest to all she loves best and no one, child or grown-up who has visited her there will ever be the same again.

Miss Hewins may have been reading or writing at her desk, she may have been solving a problem requiring hours of patient research and a sure sense of the latest authoritative statement, or again she may have been reading aloud, — the story of PERSEPHONE, if it was springtime, — or THE MAN OF SNOW, if it was near Christmas. Whatever she might be doing appeared in that setting quite the most fascinating thing in the world. Here are the books of her childhood from which she has brought forth a package to share with the readers of this little book just as she has so often shared them with groups of librarians and their friends in distant cities and towns as well as in those of Connecticut. To hear Miss Hewins recite PETER PIPER'S ALPHABET is something to remember. " It is my one parlor trick " she remarked characteristically when asked to repeat it in the children's room of the New York Public Library at the opening of the annual holiday exhibition of children's books. Needless to say it called forth tumultuous applause and every one went away determined to learn it. Here at last it is bound up with happy recollections of a delightful childhood.

ANNE CARROLL MOORE.

New York City,
Hallowe'en, 1926.

Part I: THE CHILD HERSELF

NOT every little girl lives in the house with a great-grandmother, a lively little old lady who played a very good
game of whist, a grandmother, two aunts and an uncle, besides
her father and mother. The great-grandmother tried to teach
me to knit when I was four years old, but the only result was a
distaste for knitting which I have never been able to overcome.
Perhaps it would have grown easier if she had continued the
lessons, but she went to live with another daughter when we
moved a few miles farther out of town. A great-aunt of ours
lived on the other side of Boston, and it was an event to go to
her house with our grandmother or one of our aunts for a day's
visit in the summer vacation, changing from steam-car to horse-
car, waiting at Charlestown bridge for the schooners to go
through the draw, seeing the bright red lobsters in the little
shops at each end of the bridge, and Bunker Hill monument
towering up before us. It was nearly noon when we rang the
door-bell and were greeted by her pleasant-faced maid, Joanna,
who usually told us that our aunt was out but would be in soon,
and had left word for us to make ourselves at home. In a few
minutes Joanna would come in with a large pitcher of lemonade

and a loaf of sponge-cake, such as no one but aunt could make. She had a kitchen of her own with a Brussels carpet and her own special kitchen utensils, never touched by anyone else. After we had had all the sponge-cake and lemonade we could hold, there were always two books on the parlor table to look at, one of them *The Homes of American Authors*, the other a large edition of *Lalla Rookh*, which had one of the most fiendish pictures I ever saw, illustrating " The Veiled Prophet of Khorassan." By the time the thrills attendant on this had subsided our aunt would come home, delighted to see us. It was not very long before early dinner was ready, and we were fed with delicious thick steak and water-melon, with the addition of green peas for the elders. After dinner we walked on the graveled garden paths, which have always re-called to me the lines in " O Mother dear, Jerusalem,"

> Thy gardens and thy goodly walks
> Continually are green.

There was hardly time for a visit to a little cousin across the street when we were called in to tea, and after that came leave-takings and the crown of the whole day to the two little sisters who were in the party, permission to go to the closed piano in the back parlor and choose whatever gift they liked best from those that covered the top. One was a small sugar bonnet, I remember, that lasted for years, and there were picture-books and games and all the things that children like best. I was too old for them, but one day when aunt gave me a dollar at parting I spent it on my way home for a copy of *Idylls of the King*, which I have yet.

I was born in the old town of Roxbury, now a ward of Boston. The only thing that I know about my birthplace is that there was a pond with goldfish in the garden. The house was burned before I was old enough to be taken to see it. We left it before I was two years old and went to Jamaica Plains, two or three miles farther out. There we stayed for five years, and I remember the house and garden very well. The garden was large enough for old-fashioned flowers, coreopsis, mourning bride, hollyhocks, portulaca, larkspur, monkshood and the rest, the names of which I learned as a matter of course and have never forgotten.

Then my father bought from Francis George Shaw, the father of Robert Gould Shaw, five acres of land in West Roxbury. There he liked to work on summer mornings and holidays. He had a blue smock, such as farmers used to wear, that covered him from head to foot and kept him from soiling his clothes. He planted trees of which there are one hundred and twenty left. One tree, an elm, was too large to move and remains where it was when the land was bought. A large, flowered magnolia was a great ornament to the garden which was planted after we moved to the new house. But an evergreen, over which a wistaria had run, was blown down by a severe gale and in its fall injured the magnolia seriously. The vegetable garden gave all that we could use and some for friends. In the pastures anemones bloomed on May Day, and within a short distance were hepaticas, not in large numbers but enough to give a few precious blossoms to flower lovers, who knew where to find them. An uncle of ours and one of his friends used to look for them every year, not together — for they lived several miles apart — but the first of the two to find the buds open always left his card there for the other. For years the pasture was full of fringed gentians in September and early October; but the winged seeds have a way of flying off to no one knows where, and one year there was not a plant to be seen. The next year, about a mile away, I happened to find a flourishing colony that probably sprang from the vagrant seeds, the descendants of which never came back.

Beyond this pasture were woods with Indian pipe, wild indigo, partridge berries and flowers whose names we did not know. A little farther on was what we called The Lake of the Woods. It was dry in summer, but full in spring and fall, and we always connected it with Grimm's " Iron Man," half expecting to see him come out of the water. In the swamp opposite there was a pond and a spring that flowed all winter and did not freeze solid, as was proved by a goldfish that came out of it in fine condition several months after he was put in. In the pasture our cow grazed. Her name was Jessie, which dates her to 1858 when Frémont was candidate for President. I was induced to learn to milk by the gift of a small, orange pail, but my only effort showed that " Cushy cow, bonny " would not " let down her milk " for me and that the consequence would be a smaller yield even to grown-ups and experienced handlers of kine, therefore I was not invited to milk again.

There were few entertainments for children in country villages at that time. One evening Signor Blitz with his wonderful talking dog, Bobby, and a troupe of trained canaries filled the by-no-means large Hall, and delighted every child there. After that, other " magicians " came; but not one of them was as attractive as dear Signor Blitz.

Children's parties were simple and early, from two o'clock until six on Saturdays, in Sunday clothes, with games like " Pillow," " Post Office," " Open the Gate as High as the Sky," " Uncle Johnny's Very Sick," " Hunt the Squirrel through the Wood," " I've Lost Him, I've Found Him," which can all be

From " Peter Parley's Winter Evening Tales "

[7]

played in a room without boisterous running about. Out-of-door picnics for schools were unheard of. Kissing games, which at that time were a matter of course at picnics for grown-up young folks, soon fell into disuse except in the back country.

In the summer there were two days that we longed for, and remembered with great pleasure. One was a drive to Sharon, about fifteen miles and back, to visit a great-uncle and some cousins who lived in the old farmhouse which had belonged to the family for a hundred years or more. It was a low, unpainted house with a gambrel roof, lilacs in the front yard, and a cheese room where we could follow the making from the curd to the finished product set away to ripen. Near the house was a pond where turtles sat sunning themselves on logs, and a pleasant walk through the woods around the edge of the pond, to where lady-slippers and checkerberries grew. On the way to Sharon we looked for the school children who stopped playing at recess to bow and curtsy to the strangers driving by, a mark of good manners which has unfortunately fallen into disuse in this country. It was sometimes dark before we were at home again, and I remember my first sight of a large number of fireflies dancing in a meadow, and recalled Drake's:

> Through their clustering branches dark
> Glimmers and dies the fire-fly's spark —
> Like starry twinkles that momently break
> Through the rifts of the gathering tempest's rack.

The other summer holiday was in Milton, on the eastern side of Blue Hill, where there was another farmhouse near a pond. Huckleberries grew there for anyone to pick, and we carried home all that we could use. Before we said good-by we had supper at a long table, flapjacks nearly as large as dinner plates with cider apple-sauce, which we never saw anywhere else. The old lady whose house we were in was a relation of our " Uncle John," who was not related to us except by the marriage of his brother to our aunt. He used to tell us of spending a winter there. One morning the fire was out, and he had to go half a mile to get a burning log to rekindle it. It was before matches were in general use.

We learned to watch for shadbush in bloom when the shad came into the rivers, and once, without looking for them, I found calopogon and pogonia growing in a meadow. At another time by the banks of the Charles River I walked unexpectedly close to a tall bush of pink-purple flowers that I somehow knew as Emerson's " fresh rhodora in the woods." It was the only one I ever saw in Massachusetts, but in Connecticut it is not at all uncommon. A small plant with blossoms of the same color, the fringed polygala, grew near a brook in another woodsy place, to be looked for in May. The Fourth of July was the time to expect the white azalea and water lilies that grew near the river. Every month had its own wild flowers, up to November, when witch-hazel bloomed " like a gleam of pale sunshine " — as one nature-lover describes it.

Apple and pear time in the fall was always welcomed. We knew the names of the pears, Louise Bonne, Seckel, Beurre d'Anjou, Clapp's Favorite, Beurre Bosc, Flemish Beauty and the rest that our father had planted. Some of the apple trees, Red Astrachan, Snow, Baldwin, Russet, Greening, were on the land when we bought it, and we helped in the picking and the packing in barrels.

The County Agricultural Society had a fair every September in a large building and grounds in Dedham. We all went, as a matter of course, and visited the spading contests, where a skillful Irishman, Dennis Doody by name, always came out at the head. Then we visited the horses and cattle, and ended in the hall where the vegetables, fruit, patchwork quilts and fancy-work were on exhibition. In the afternoon there were horse races and, once certainly, a baseball game. I went to see it from school without luncheon, and distinguished myself by fainting in the hot sun.

Of children of my own age I knew very little. One or two in the neighborhood used to come to play with me, and a cousin lived not far away. But, not going to school, I did not learn out-of-door games and had more spare time than if I had been in the schoolroom morning and afternoon. There were no kinder-gartens then on this side of the Atlantic. If there had been, I should have known many things that I have never learned.

It was in the early fifties that my mother taught me to read and spell. I do not remember the process, but I have no knowl-edge of a time when the words in an ordinary printed book and the marriages, deaths and accidents in the *Boston Evening Transcript* were beyond my powers of pronouncing and under-standing. *My First School Book* was the means of an easy and pleasant acquaintance with print. My copy disappeared long ago; but in a collection of school books within my reach is one much fresher and less used, from which I am able to renew my acquaintance with " The Disobedient Rabbit " and the two boys, one selfish and one generous, who had nine-pence each to spend on Fourth of July. One ate up his very soon, but the other one proved his altruistic character by spend-ing half of his wealth for an orange to give to a sick friend. *Emerson's First Part*, a simple little arithmetic, had pictures to beguile young mathematicians along the difficult paths of ad-dition, subtraction, multiplication and division, with sometimes

3

Twice 1 are 2.

This book is something new.

From MARMADUKE MULTIPLY.

(*See page 38*)

a short story like this: "When Nathaniel was sick, one of his schoolmates brought him four grapes, but his physician said that he must eat only one at a time. How many times could he eat one before they were all gone?" The little book ended with the multiplication table up to twelve times twelve. I never saw afterward an arithmetic for school use made enticing with pictures.

There must have been picture books given me in my early

days that went the way of most paper-covered books for children. I remember dimly one about a wood-cutter, but it was not Red Riding Hood. The pictures of that date were usually very crude, colored by hand with a generous bestowal of vermilion, Prussian blue, gamboge and crimson lake that overflowed the edges of the children's garments. A little earlier the colors were put on by boys and girls, each of whom was responsible for only one tint before passing on a picture to the next in order.

The school where my brother and I went was first in a large, sunny room in an old-fashioned house where an old lady, known as Aunt Electa, was kindness itself to the children, especially if they had fallen or had any of the various pains and aches that children have. After a year or two the school was moved to a small building farther away from the village street, and remained there until the teacher was married and went to Europe for a year before going to live in Boston.

There was a little girl in the class above me who was a bookworm and had the run of two libraries, one a minister's, the other the property of a leading Boston publisher. We came together like " halves of one dissevered world " and what one had not read the other had, from Miss Yonge's *Daisy Chain* to Edgar Allan Poe.

One day a pleasant white-haired man came to our house to sell some books he had written. His name was Warren Burton, and he was well known as a teacher until he retired. One of the books, *The District School as it Was*, was a favorite of mine and I lived over the life of the boys and girls in the little red schoolhouse, from three years old to the nearly grown-up pupils of the winter months, the teachers, from dear Mary Smith to the pompous or ineffective college students, and the champion speller who understood an order from the master to " go and spell Jonas " — who was splitting wood — to mean that he was to give him all the hard words in the spelling book and report on those he missed. An " exhibition " was a festive occasion to them, with " pieces " spoken and, once in a while, a dialogue or a scene from a play enacted on a stage curtained with checked blankets and lighted by candles or oil lamps.

This country school was of the late twenties or early thirties. Some improvements had been made in schoolhouses before 1850, but they had none of the luxuries of to-day. There were no swimming pools, gymnasiums, folk-dances, library books, luncheon counters, pianos, fire-drills, sewing, graduation presents, talks about books or pictures, celebrations of Christmas or other holidays, or manual training. Children had less " homework " than they do now, and life was not as hurried. Country boys and girls had chores to do at home that kept them busy a part of out-of-school hours, and made them grow up under a sense of responsibility. Girls had washing dishes, sweeping, dusting and keeping rooms in order; the boys shoveling snow, feeding horses, cows and poultry, and doing errands. In most families the girls did a " stint " of sewing every day, and some of them cross-stitched the alphabet large and small, the figures up to ten, and their name and age in bright-colored wools on canvas, the elaborate and dismal samplers of years before having gone out of fashion. Their place was taken by slippers in cross-stitch and crocheted bags of twine for carrying luncheons and other school properties, in addition to a book or two. Sewing was not taught in country schools, and cooking was an unheard-of part of the curriculum. If a girl liked to cook there were opportunities for her in the home kitchen.

One of my earliest remembrances is of sitting in front of a soft-coal fire and hearing " Flow gently, sweet Afton " sung.

After I had learned to read, the singer, an aunt who died before I was six, must have shown me the song in her little fine-print, gilt-edged Burns with a black and gold cover, for I should hardly have found it for myself. There were a great many words in the book that I had never seen, but a glossary at the end told me what they meant and I read some of the poems over and over, till before I or anyone else knew what I was doing I was able to read Lowland Scotch easily, and never had to stumble over it in later years.

I was about seven when I was taken to hear a trained orchestra and Camilla Urso, then a girl of fourteen or so, with braids of hair down her back, who played the violin wonderfully. It was something to remember, everyone said. Applause, which I had never heard before, frightened me at first, until I understood what it was. There were no children's concerts in those days, and I did not hear any great music again for several years.

The first play that I remember seeing was *Cinderella*, though my impressions of it are fragmentary, chiefly of the fairies in spangled white and of Pedro's funny tricks. The next play was *The Midsummer Night's Dream*, which I did not read until after seeing it.

In those days anyone who was on Boston Common on May Day could see groups of girls in white muslin, usually with a boy as King of the May. There must have been many colds and attacks of pneumonia for the rest of the month. The first May Day party that I ever went to was in the large parlor of a neighbor's house. It was given for the hostess's niece who had been ill the winter before, and had been promised a May party by her aunt if she would get well in time for it. A tall Maypole stood in the middle of the room, and every girl but one had a wreath of arbutus — she was a little older than the others and wore a wreath of pansies. I think that the boys had wreaths, but am not quite sure. I kept mine quite dry for several years. The party was over at sunset, and everyone went home happy. May parties were not uncommon, though a Massachusetts May is, as Lowell said, "more like mayn't." The schools of to-day have found it wiser to crown their May Queens later in the month.

At one of the simple afternoon parties a sea captain, whose home was in the neighborhood, and who had just landed from a long voyage, came in with something new and strange in his hand — a stereoscope and a few views at which we were all invited to look. The only one that I remember distinctly is Notre Dame. It was not long before we had a stereoscope of our own, with views of Tintern Abbey and other delightful places that were soon as familiar as if we had really seen them.

In the early fifties Christmas trees were not common. Stockings were hung on Christmas Eve and filled with small presents, including candy animals; but the family celebration was later in the day. The first Christmas tree that any of us ever saw was a hat-tree covered with pine branches and hung with toys, books and whatever children would like best. Santa Claus came with it to distribute the gifts, though his call was short on account of the many homes that he had to visit. I remember that there were waiting for me a doll's iron bedstead, with beautifully made sheets and blankets, a wax doll beautifully dressed, a gold pencil and a silver fruit-knife which I have to this day.

One year, when I was twelve or thirteen, a family in the neighborhood persuaded a dancing teacher to open a class in the hall which was our only place for lectures, concerts or dances. There were about a dozen girls to every boy. The teacher was a woman of mature years with carefully woven hair on each side of her face, a black silk gown, and very neat feet in black silk stockings and slippers. The Varsovienne, the Polka, Redowa and other dances of the period were taught us as well as the Lancers, other "square cotillions" and some of the old-fashioned country dances. At the end of the quarter there was an exhibition in the evening when the girls all wore their prettiest dresses. Mine was a low-necked, sky-blue barège with a tucked skirt, a sash of the same color, and hot-house flowers at the back of my head.

Adelina Patti was seventeen, I thirteen, when I listened for the first time to an opera, *Don Giovanni*, sung by the finest voice I have ever heard. Patti was lovely to look upon, and one of the papers said that when she danced with the tenor it was like an elephant turning round a gazelle. I never wished to hear her after her voice broke, and I have always remembered her as I heard her that Saturday afternoon in the Boston Theatre.

In the middle of the century the Warren Street Chapel was much like the modern settlement. The Reverend Charles Francis Barnard made it a church for children, and gave them opportunities of seeing good pictures and statues. Because there were dancing classes in the chapel, he was known as " the dancing parson." He formed the idea of engaging the Music Hall for May Day with an orchestra to play, and letting the children dance as much as they pleased. We used to go with a group of other girls, sometimes under the care of one mother, again with two or three. There were tableaux in a small hall on a lower floor, flowers and ice cream for sale, and it was altogether a very pleasant day to remember. A remembrance of the Music Hall even earlier is of going to one of the horticultural exhibitions when I could not have been more than three or four years old. One of the party opened by mistake the door of a room where a committee of white-haired gentlemen was deciding on prizes for grapes and pears. I began to cry when no one offered me even a taste of one, and the door was hastily shut behind us.

Schoolrooms of those days were bare and uninviting compared with their modern successors. Our high school was in a hall the use of which for town meetings gave us three days' holidays, " one to make ready," the second for the meeting and the third for cleaning. On a raised platform on one side was a large glass case of apparatus used to illustrate what is now called physics. There was not a photograph of any famous building, picture or statue in the room. Equipment was of the simplest and most meagre, but the teaching was so thorough that I have never forgotten Latin or French irregular verbs, and can read the two languages at sight as well as I ever could.

My high-school diploma was given me, and then, because I was younger than the other graduates, and colleges for girls were in their infancy, it was a puzzle what to do with me next. The Girls' High and Normal School, as it was called, in Boston was highly recommended. I passed the examination on one of the rainiest days of my life, and was admitted. It was not easy to adjust myself to the conditions there, in a class of sixty or seventy girls who had had public-school training from the beginning; but I floundered along somehow and kept my head above water, although my marks were not high. The normal training was for the most part obtained by the Squeers method of substituting in the schools where a teacher was ill or absent for any reason, and we had no lectures on pedagogy.

Before long I began to make friends with a few girls who were

Darley invent et sculpt

Printed by James E. Major

Etching by Felix O. C. Darley for Washington Irving's
"The Legend of Sleepy Hollow"

lovers of literature, and they introduced me to *Water Babies*, *Marjorie Fleming* and other books that have lived for more than half a century. The class had free discussion in the English literature hours, and gained the habit of talking easily and to the point, though some views were original — to say the least. When we were reading Gray's " Elegy " one of the girls insisted that " the little tyrant of the fields " was some small animal, like a weasel or a fox.

Another habit, unusual in schools of that date, was connected with our study of history. We had " date-books " in which we wrote from dictation brief histories of reigns, to be learned for the next lesson, in addition to a full account of an earlier reign from books at home, in the public library, the good school library or anywhere else. I read French more easily than most of the girls, and quite as often took the history of a reign from a book of that language on the school shelves as from histories in English.

The " Elegy " followed Gray's *Bard* and preceded *Hamlet*, which led to many long discussions over sentences and phrases not easy to understand. We had not much practice in writing English. I cannot remember writing more than one theme, or " composition," as it was called in those days. A list of subjects was read aloud and the girls chose what they liked best or thought easiest, without consulting a teacher. When the teacher read the essays she went over her corrections or suggestions with every girl; but there was no practice in the use of words as there is now. The girls learned some things thoroughly, but could go through a four years' course without any real training in the English that is now a favorite elective in college.

The school year ended and most of the class began teaching in the graded schools. About a dozen stayed for the advanced year of languages, psychology or mental philosophy as it was called then. There were one or two other studies which I have forgotten, except chemistry, which nearly blew me up one day. The writing habit was encouraged by what were called " special exercises," when after weeks of hard work had brought forth a paper on some literary or scientific subject, the author or compiler was invited to read it in the school hall to an admiring audience from all the classes.

The school had invitations to hear and see the favorite musicians of the time, one of whom — Teresa Carreño — was a child-wonder from South America who played remarkably on a grand piano in Music Hall. The schools gave a concert in the same hall for the officers of a Russian warship that was anchored at a Boston dock for a short time. In return they invited the schools to visit the ship on a specified day. The school principals agreed that a general invitation would bring too great a crowd, and that it would be better to limit the guests to the graduating classes in the high schools. It was a cloudless day in late June or early July, for the summer vacation did not begin until after the middle of the month. The ship was spotless, and the officers were in equally immaculate uniforms. There were flowers everywhere, and later a delicious luncheon was served. Some of the officers spoke excellent English, and those who did not made themselves understood by gestures or French phrases. The ship's band played for dancing on deck. It was the first time that the girls had met foreign naval officers and they never forgot them. A member of one of the graduating classes and the most attractive girl in it was escorted home by her partner in the dance, and was an object of envy. Altogether, it was a delightful day and a pleasant ending to our school life.

Our schoolhouse had once been a medical college — of some

notoriety from the murder of Dr. Parkman by Dr. Webster and the discovery of his remains in the furnace by the janitor, who showed in evidence a set of false teeth identified by the dentist who made them. The basement and cellar were ghastly enough to be the scene of any crime. The house was in Mason Street, just around the corner from West Street and the stately houses of Colonnade Row, at the window of one of which a white-haired gentleman used to sit, the youngest son of Paul Revere and the father of two sons killed in the Civil War.

My grown-up library began with the first edition of Hawthorne's *Marble Faun* and was soon increased by Longfellow's *Golden Legend*, a blue and gold Tennyson and Jean Paul's *Titan* in two thick volumes, which I have never found interesting. Palgrave's *Golden Treasury* is a book that I bought at about the same time, and I never look at it without a feeling of thankfulness that I own it. Pope's *Homer* and Wright's *Dante* have Flaxman's outlines to add to their interest, and I was familiar with the pictures in both before my high-school days. I had had very little public-school training and was at a disadvantage in much of the new work, but an acquaintance with the Greek and Roman gods and goddesses and the Siege of Troy besides the habit of looking up subjects in the *Encyclopædia Britannica* kept me from absolute ignorance. I know something of great artists and their paintings. Pictures and statues with stories always appealed to me — such as Crawford's Orpheus, Virgil and Dante meeting the Latin poets and the Scheffer Dante and Beatrice. I knew the Flaxman outlines in the Wright translation of *Dante*, and also in Pope's *Homer*, and the floating figures of Paolo and Francesca on the library wall of a Dante scholar.

One-fourth of the boys in the High School, taken in alphabetical order, " spoke a piece " every Friday. The girls, although they mounted the platform to read what were then called " compositions," were not expected to repeat in public the poetry that they learned, but were permitted to say it at the noon hour or at other odd times to a teacher in the privacy of a class-room. In four years a girl could commit to memory and make her own forty poems she had herself selected, and of any length she pleased. In this way I learned many lines of Longfellow, Tennyson and Scott and some poems of Milton, Bryant and Whittier. One Christmas I was given a copy of *L'Allegro*, illustrated and without notes, and I learned it by heart with the enjoyment which a girl can never feel who reads it for the first time in " College English " requirements, where Cerberus, the Styx, the Graces, May Day, the skylark, Queen Mab and Robin Goodfellow are supposedly unknown and carefully explained.

In West Roxbury there had been a small library in a room leading out of " Betsy's " country store, where she sold a varied assortment of goods from molasses to calico. The library had been closed for many years, but at the beginning of my last year at school it was moved to a room not much larger, that was used, when necessary, for a dressing room at dances in the hall which it adjoined. This library was remarkably well chosen and had received many gifts from Theodore Parker during his ministry in the old white church not far away. It was kept alive by annual dollar subscriptions, and cared for by an old gentleman and his wife who were " uncle " and " aunty " to all the children in the neighborhood. They bought the books, prepared them for circulation, made the fires in the stove all through the winter months, repaired loose leaves and bindings and were at their posts every Monday for fifty weeks in the year. They gave their services freely, but after a while the circulation increased and an assistant was employed at twenty-five dollars a year, afterwards increased to fifty.

Everyone in town regardless of church or political affiliations would help the library, and though the actual assets were not large judged by city standards, they meant a great deal to us. Various entertainments were given for it, fairs, suppers, a Dickens party, an exhibition of antiques, tableaux with negro spirituals sung between, led by a woman who had given years of service in the South Sea islands. When the librarian and his wife were on vacation it fell to me, as secretary of the Library Association, to charge and discharge the books in a ledger under the names of the readers. The pleasure of knowing the library well enough to find books easily was increased by the treasures on the shelves, unnoticed by most of the readers, Ben Jonson, Leigh Hunt, George Sand's *Consuelo* in the translation by Francis George Shaw and first published in the Brook Farm paper, the *Harbinger*, Carlyle's translation of *Wilhelm Meister* and *German Romance*, with the eerie " Golden Jar," some of Tieck's fairy tales and Jean Paul's *Quintus Fixlein*.

An English neighbor who went home for a visit brought back a collection of three-volume novels for the library. They were received with some doubt and looked over carefully before they were admitted to the shelves, but I never heard any objections made to them, though they were probably the work of second or third class authors. Some of the families in the town finally decided that the library would be more used in a more central position, and it was moved into a room a little larger than its former home, and made free to all the inhabitants of that part of the town — men, women and children.

There was a reading club in our village after the free library opened, and once or twice in the winter the members used to impersonate the characters from some favorite author. Once we had a Mother Goose party, when one lady made a great success as:

My mother's maid,
She stole oranges, I'm afraid,
Some in her pocket and some in her sleeve;
She stole oranges, I do believe.

Wherever she was she dropped an orange. We had a great stuffed goose, though I cannot remember where we borrowed it. I was so worn out with reading notes of regret that I did not care what I stood for, and with a sad countenance and a dismal gown I answered the doorbell as " The maiden all forlorn," which made some of the guests think that something serious had happened to one of the family.

My twenty-first birthday was an unusual day for October, almost as warm as midsummer with nasturtiums untouched by frost, and cut in long trails to decorate the house for a Dickens party. My father, as Mr. Wardle, received the guests the first part of the evening, and later appeared as Alfred Jingle. I had asked not to have it entirely a young party and, on that account, the characters were played with much more spirit than if the parts had been taken by boys and girls. It made no difference whether they had ever met before or not. They recognized each other as kindred spirits. Captain Cuttle and Jack Bunsby brought down the house by dancing a " fore and after." Sairey Gamp did not know that Betsey Prig would be there but when they saw each other their only regret was that Mrs. Harris had not been invited. Dolly Varden and her mother were in evidence, Dolly with her hair elaborately dressed by a kind neighbor. Betsey Trotwood was there and the faithful Janet, Sam Weller and Bob Sawyer, Lizzie Hexam and the Doll's Dressmaker, Mrs. Jarley and Little Nell. I wish that we had kept a list of the characters, for some of them have entirely gone from my memory.

The next morning was dark and cold and rainy. The nasturtiums were all frost-bitten in the night. But the fun and unexpectedness of the party remained with all who were present.

From " Grandmamma's Book of Rhymes for the Nursery "

Part II: HER BOOKS

LOOKING back into the early fifties, I can see as plainly as
any of the faces of family or friends the big, unwieldy,
two-volume Froissart in a faded purplish binding with a gilt
knight on horseback on the cover, and pictures of ladies in lit-
ters and processions of knights and soldiers that I loved to look
at, and the fat one-volume edition of Gibbon in figure much like
the author. Both books must have been too tall for the bookcase shelves, because they were on the table between the front
windows. In the room where they lived I was discovered one
Sunday afternoon reading Godey's *Lady's Book* which, although extremely mild and harmless, was thought in those days
a little grown-up for a person of four and a half. The next day I
was taken into town and made the proud owner of a copy of
Jacob Abbott's *Lucy's Conversations*, my first bound book,
which I have to this day, with my name and the date in it. It is
in this book that Lucy has croup in the night and the next
morning is given a powder in jelly and a roasted apple that was

cooked by hanging it in front of the fire from a string held by a flatiron on the mantelpiece.

The other Lucy books followed in due time, at intervals of a few months. Was there ever a more delightful journey than that which Lucy was invited to make to the seashore with her friend Marielle and Marielle's mother, the mysterious Lady Jane who " came from some foreign country " ? How grand it was for the little girls to travel in a carriage, to have tea by themselves in Lady Jane's sister's library, waited on by a black serving man, and to look at drawers of curiosities, shells and minerals and a picture in mosaic of a burning mountain, by way of entertainment! *Lucy in the Mountains* is not nearly as impressive or awe-inspiring; but the stay at the General's and his monthly inspection of everything in the house and farm buildings, ending with a round cake for every one of the children, lingers in my memory together with the " beautiful little apple pie " in *Lucy's Stories* and other food described with the detail which Jacob Abbott knew children love. An American family as simple and happy was described in *Clara's Amusements* by Mrs. Anna Bache of Philadelphia, a descendant of Benjamin Franklin, who in her preface says that she has seen the plan of parents interesting themselves in their children's recreations " acted out with success in a family of small means and simple habits." The children played Robinson Crusoe. Their father and mother told them about the French Revolution, showed them pictures of Robin Hood and King Alfred and taught them how to make scrapbooks, play games and guess riddles. They learned, too, from their mother's example to be good neighbors and help her cook for a poor, sick woman, and to make her more comfortable. In all this there was no self-righteousness, but a perfectly natural and wholesome spirit.

It could not have been long after this that Lane's three-volume *Arabian Nights*, with Harvey's illustrations, came to a shelf in the grown-up bookcase, not too high for small hands to reach. I did not read "Aladdin" or " The Forty Thieves " for several years, because they were not in Lane's edition, but long before I had ever seen or heard of them Sinbad the Sailor, the Flying Horse, Bedreddin Hassan, one-eyed calenders, dervishes, afrites, genii, gazelles and ghouls were as well known to me as the Mother Goose people or Lucy and her family.

I have now two books that were given me for Christmas just after I was six years old. They have never lost their charm. One is *Gockel and Scratchfoot*, or *The History of Two Little Chickens* from the German of G. Süs, published in a square octavo by Willis P. Hazard of Philadelphia, with full-page lithographs very well drawn and hand colored — the miller's wife feeding her poultry, the visit of Scratchfoot to her aunt, the duck, and the triumphant return of the two lost chickens in a flower-decked basket carried by Henry and Christina, the brother and sister who had found them in the wood. Within a few years I have seen in a German bookseller's catalogue a picture of this author, Gustav Süs, with his two children. He was of the Düsseldorf School, and an artist of some reputation as well as a story-teller and writer.

The other book is *The Man of Snow* by Harriet Myrtle (Mrs. Hugh Miller, wife of the geologist), one of a series of three, telling the simple, happy life of a family, father, mother and little girl, who go from London to live in a cottage in the country. *The Man of Snow* is the record of a joyous Christmas time, when the mother tells little Mary and her two boy cousins about the funny things that happened to a snow man when she was a child.

K was the Kitchen, where the
supper was cooked,
But none of the visitors into it looked.

From "Alderman's Feast"

Many of the picture books of the fifties were published in
Albany by Sprague or by Fisk and Little, hand colored or rather
hand daubed, and in pasteboard covers. The best of them all
was *The Alderman's Feast* because it told so much about
London. The city's name is not mentioned in the book, but
somehow I knew where to find Bow Church and the " yeomen
so stout and tall, in scarlet and gold," and I looked forward to
the time when I should really see them. With the Aldermen
and Dick Whittington for friends, what wonder that Bow
Church was as familiar a building as the Boston State House?

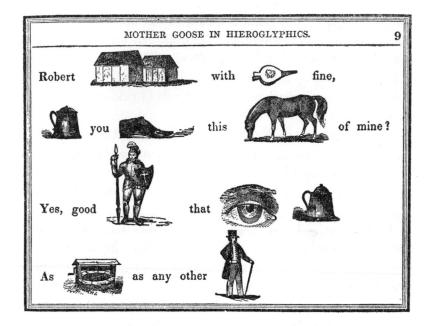

Robert [barns] with [bellows] fine,

[tankard] you [shoe] this [horse] of mine?

Yes, good [sir] that [eye] [can]

As [well] as any other [man]

Besides, its bells were ringing in " Oranges and Lemons " in our *Mother Goose*, of which there were two editions that we learned by heart. One was a reprint of the little square " only pure edition " first issued by Munroe and Francis in 1833 with wood cuts, many of them English, some with suggestions of Bewick and his school. The other was *Mother Goose in Hieroglyphics*, published by Appleton in 1849, an auction copy, more tattered and torn than the man in " The House that Jack Built." The poem runs thus:

> Robert (Barns) with (bellows) fine
> (Can) you (shoe) this (horse) of mine?
> Yes, good (Sir), that (I can)
> As (well) as any other (man),

the words in parentheses being represented by pictures, easy

[31]

to guess except " Sir," who is a man in full armor with shield, lance and plumed helmet. The beginning of my acquaintance with *Mother Goose* was from this book. The other came later. The habit of guessing the pictures had always helped me in solving puzzles in magazines, in all kinds of riddles and in digging out allusions.

I know that my mother taught me to read out of *My First School Book* because I remember the book afterward, but I have no idea how I learned the letters unless I picked them up from blocks or, as one of the family did later, got them from the names blown in glass bottles.

Back as far as I can remember any books I can see an old *Æsop's Fables*, coverless and titleless, with long s's and old wood cuts. It was Croxall's translation into eighteenth century English with " applications," not " morals " attached, which sometimes were as entertaining as the fables and the cuts. It is uncertain who the illustrator was, whether Kirkall or another, but Bewick followed him closely in his cuts for *Æsop*. The pictures of the gods and goddesses of Roman mythology in the sky, with Juno attended by her peacock, or the more homely scenes like " The Stag in the Ox-Stall " or " The Nurse and the Wolf " were as interesting to me as they were to the children of two or three generations before, who had read and owned the book. There is very plain English in the Fables, and words not now heard in the polite world are freely used, but I am sure that I was never the worse for them.

Maria Edgeworth's stories, prosaic as they seem to twentieth-century schoolgirls, are of a pleasant family life where mother, father and children have the same interests. If the mother and father went to pay a visit the children went, too, and by this means met people worth knowing. The Edgeworths' friends

FAB. LXXVII. *The* Fox *and the* Vizor-mask.

FAB. CXVI. *The* Wolf *and the* Kid.

From Croxall's translation of "Aesop's Fables"

[33]

and family connections — the Wedgwoods, the Darwins and others — were all in advance of their time, inventors or men of science, and it is life with such families that Harry and Lucy, Frank and Rosamond knew. They always had something to do and to think of — riddles, puzzles and nonsense. Their study of history was made real by games like " Contemporaries," and they were taught to learn poetry and to connect it with history or science.

Jacob Abbott's *Rollo* Books and *Franconia* Stories are full of practical good sense in dealing with children and in suggesting occupations for them. One of these occupations, letter writing, had an unexpected result when Phonny let his imagination run away with him in describing the supposed burning of his mother's house and barn, and the letter was mailed by mistake, bringing Beechnut home from Boston in the middle of a rainy night to find house and farm buildings in their usual condition.

The "Aimwell " series, published in the fifties, had the same ideals of family life. The children and the older folks on a Vermont farm had a family paper, learned to guess riddles and puzzles, and played memory games. It was from one of these books and also from *My Favorite Picture Book*, a collection of pictures by Birket Foster, Harrison Weir, " Phiz " and other English illustrators, that I was once able to answer a request in the *American Journal of Folklore* for " The Peter Piper Alphabet," and afterward to have a pleasant meeting with the family who asked for it.

Lydia Maria Child, whose *Juvenile Miscellany* died about the time that the *Rollo* Books began, had republished many of her stories in *Flowers for Children*. In 1855 she issued her last book for them, although she wrote several stories for

THE COCOA-MAN.

OLD POLYPOD.

From " Beechnut, A Franconia Story " by Jacob Abbott

[35]

Our Young Folks between 1865 and 1869. Her *New Flowers for Children* has one of her most charming tales, " The Royal Rosebud," the story of the little princess, Edward IV's youngest daughter, whose mother in the troubled times after the king's death, made her a nun as the safest way of disposing of her. Mrs. Child's *Girls' Own Book* taught me many games and riddles, English and French. Her *Frugal Housewife* was full of the industrious, thrifty New England spirit which, carried into her simple living, enabled her to give sums out of all proportion to her income to philanthropic societies.

Translations from the German were in fashion at this time. It was through German that Mary Howitt had introduced Hans Andersen to English readers about 1845. Some of her translations, by no means exact, had been published by Wiley and Putnam in a little square book with colored illustrations in 1847. It was in a gift book called *Christmas Roses* which belonged to Jenny across the street that I first read " Ole Luckoie," " Little Ida's Flowers " and " The Nightingale." " Ole Luckoie " with its wonderful journeys under the umbrella of the Danish Sandman was the favorite, and there is no translation as good of one of the couplets which the lead pencil made for the doll's wedding:

> Her skin it is made of a white kid glove,
> And on her he looks with an eye of love.

It must have been two or three years after this, when it was an event for one's father to go all the way to New York, that Jenny's father brought her from there a fat, green-covered Andersen with the creepy " Travelling Companion," " The Little Red Shoes," " The Little Mermaid " and all the other stories. She had another book, too, even fatter, that I tried to

Illustration by Millais from " Lilliput Levee "

find for years and at last traced as *The Child's Own Book,*
published by Munroe and Francis. An advertisement at the
end of *The Boys' Story Book* issued in 1845 says, " The tales
have all their original beauty unimpaired; nothing changed
except any vulgar or improper expression unfit for the juvenile
reader." How the titles " Griselda," " Jack and the Beanstalk,"
" Peronella," " Riquet with the Tuft," " Fortunio," even " Cinderella," bring back the little pictures of beauteous ladies in
short-waisted gowns, and the amateur dramatized versions of
" Bluebeard " and " Fatal and Fortune " performed in the barn
by some venerable persons of sixteen and eighteen before an
admiring audience of fewer years! How the book recalls, too,
the glorious Hall of Mirrors in " The Invisible Prince " and
Bluet, the Princess' cat, deprived of his food by the supposedly
invisible Leandor in full sight of the audience, in all the beauty
of his blue and silver doublet and white-plumed hat.

Grimm's Fairy Tales, although they were published in 1853
by C. S. Francis in a very good two-volume translation with
Wehnert's illustrations, did not come into the house until
nearly ten years later and stayed for only a short time, for the
precious copy was sent by the owner, a younger sister, to the
soldiers in the hospitals as the dearest thing she could give to
her country.

Munroe and Francis were the American publishers of *Marmaduke Multiply,* who made even the multiplication table
amusing and easy to learn. Is it possible to forget " Five times
twelve are sixty," illustrated by a sour-faced woman picking her
steps over a threshold and saying, " This house is like a pigsty,"
or " Four times eight are thirty-two," where a very fat, waddling
person exclaims, " I once could dance as well as you," or " Seven
times eight are fifty-six," where a boy is running away after

having broken the toy cart belonging to another who, instead of running after him and giving him what he deserves, is merely standing in a wooden attitude and saying, " That fellow merits twenty kicks " ?

From " Grandmamma's Book of Rhymes for the Nursery "

The Wonder Book was on my pillow when I opened my eyes on the morning of my seventh birthday. The purple-covered *Tanglewood Tales* with Proserpine and Europa, Theseus, Jason and Circe is still mine; but the dear green *Wonder Book* with the Hammatt Billings pictures of the groups of children on Tanglewood porch, Perseus holding up the Gorgon's head, King Midas, Pandora, the three Golden Apples, Baucis and Philemon and the Chimera vanished long years ago, and not even the Walter Crane or Maxfield Parrish editions will ever take its place.

I had read, skipping the moralizing, a little old *Robinson Crusoe* in the house, with yellow paper and small type. But I never really loved it as I loved a book that was brought me from New York about this time — *The Swiss Family Robinson*

— their suggestive makeshifts and picknicky ways of living in tent, tree and cavern, their pet monkey and all the fauna and flora of the remarkable island which combined the vegetation of the tropical and the temperate zones, and where everyone could do and find just the right thing in an emergency.

Grace Greenwood (Sara Lippincott) had written *Recollections of My Childhood* and *History of My Pets* a few years before this time. The stories in the first are often sentimental, but the account of her child life in western New York is most amusing. Her monthly paper, *The Little Pilgrim*, published in Philadelphia, came to me through the mail, and I had the pleasure of going to the post office to get it and of reading her stories of history and travel, which made Shakespeare, Scott and Byron, the royal prisoner, James I of Scotland, Jane Beaufort and Catherine Douglas, Guy of Warwick and Sir Philip Sydney real living persons whose homes I looked forward to seeing some day.

Shakespeare was not my " daily food," but there were two books illustrated with the steel engravings of the time that led me to him. They were in the parlor where we sat on Sunday afternoons, and were an unfailing source of pleasure. One of them was a large edition of Mrs. Jameson's *Characteristics of Women*. From the faces, sad like Ophelia, mirthful like Beatrice, frowning like Lady Macbeth, or merely pretty and meaningless like Perdita and Miranda, I began to read what the book had to say about them, and after a while the plays themselves. The only Shakespeare girls that I had ever seen — Helena and Hermia — were not in the *Characteristics* at all. And when I saw them in *Midsummer Night's Dream* they were overshadowed by the clowns and the fairies. The other book, Allan Cunningham's *Gallery of Pictures*, had some of

THE LITTLE PILGRIM.

Edited by Grace Greenwood.

VOL. II.]   PHILADELPHIA, JANUARY, 1855.   [No. 1.

THE LITTLE PILGRIM,
A MONTHLY JOURNAL FOR
GIRLS AND BOYS.
EDITED BY
GRACE GREENWOOD & LEANDER K. LIPPINCOTT.

TERMS.—Fifty Cents a year for a single copy, or Ten copies for Four Dollars—*payable in advance.*

☞ Articles for THE LITTLE PILGRIM to be addressed, *post-paid*, to GRACE GREENWOOD, Philadelphia.

JOHN ANDREW.

WRITTEN FOR THE LITTLE PILGRIM.

THE BAREFOOT BOY.

BY JOHN G. WHITTIER.

BLESSINGS on thee, little man,
Barefoot boy, with cheek of tan!
With thy turned-up pantaloons,
And thy merry-whistled tunes—
With thy red lip, redder still
Kissed by strawberries on the hill—
With the sunshine on thy face,
Through thy torn brim's jaunty grace:
From my heart I give thee joy,
I was once a barefoot boy!

Prince thou art—the grown-up man
Only is republican.
Let the million-dollared ride—
Barefoot, trudging at his side,
Thou hast more than he can buy,
In the reach of ear and eye—
Outward sunshine, inward joy:
Blessings on thee, barefoot boy!

Oh! for boyhood's painless play,
Sleep that wakes in laughing day,
Health that mocks the doctor's rules,
Knowledge, never learned of schools,
Of the wild bee's morning chase,
Of the wild flower's time and place,

Flight of fowl, and habitude
Of the tenants of the wood,
How the tortoise bears his shell,
How the wood-chuck digs his cell,
And the ground-mole sinks his well;
How the robin feeds her young,
How the oriole's nest is hung;
Where the whitest lilies blow,
Where the freshest berries grow,
Where the ground-nut trails its vine,
Where the wood-grape's clusters shine;
Of the black wasp's cunning way,
Mason of his walls of clay,
And the architectural plans
Of grey hornet artizans!—
For, eschewing books and tasks,
Nature answers all he asks;
Hand in hand with her he walks,
Face to face with her he talks,
Part and parcel of her joy,—
Blessings on the barefoot boy!

Oh! for boyhood's time of June,
Crowding years in one brief moon,
When all things I heard or saw,
Me, their master, waited for.
I was rich in flowers and trees,
Humming birds and honey bees;
For my sport the squirrel played,
Plied the snouted mole his spade;
For my taste the blackberry cone
Purpled over hedge and stone;
Laughed the brook for my delight
Through the day, and through the night,
Whispering at the garden wall,
Talked with me from fall to fall;
Mine the sand-rimmed pickerel pond,
Mine the walnut slopes beyond,
Mine on bending orchard trees
Apples of Hesperides!
Still as my horizon grew,
Larger grew my riches too;
All the world I saw or knew
Seemed a complex Chinese toy
Fashioned for a barefoot boy!

Oh! for festal dainties spread,
Like my bowl of milk and bread,—
Pewter spoon and bowl of wood,
On the door-stone grey and rude!
O'er me, like a regal tent,
Cloudy-ribbed the sunset bent,
Purple-curtained, fringed with gold,
Looped in many a wind-swung fold;
While for music came the play
Of the pied frog's orchestra;

the old Boydell prints — Reynolds's Puck, Henry V before Honfleur, the Duke of Rutland, Kemble as Hamlet, Henry VIII and Anne Boleyn and Hero and Ursula watching for Beatrice in the pleached bower. In that, or more probably in a portfolio of prints cut from magazines, were Anne Page and Slender and Christopher Sly in the palace. These all gave me a bowing acquaintance with Shakespeare characters, though for some time, two or three years perhaps, the *Midsummer Night's Dream* was the only play that I really read. The portraits of the great actors, Kemble as Hamlet and Mrs. Siddons as the Tragic Muse, in the *Gallery of Pictures* fascinated me and made me wish to know more about them and their lives. I had not been in a real theater more than three or four times, but I loved the stage and anything about actors, always reading over and over the advertisements of plays at the theaters in Boston, knowing the names and who acted in them. The first life of anyone that I ever read, except perhaps Abbott's *Josephine, Madame Roland* and *Marie Antionette*, was a book that has never lost its charm — Mrs. *Mowatt's Autobiography of an Actress*. I was interested in her life in the old French château, the plays acted by the large family of children there, and later in New York, the runaway marriage, the happy country life afterward, and the play-acting that had been a pleasure and a recreation for the young wife and her sisters turned into a means of support when her husband lost his fortune.

Among the Sunday afternoon books were volumes of the *London Art Journal* that had, besides copies of a great many early Victorian pictures and statues of no great merit, some old Italian masters and more from Van Dyck, Reynolds, Gainsborough and Turner. With them and the Cunningham *Gal-*

lery as companions, it was like going home to go into the
National Gallery and find the Titian " Bacchus and Ariadne "
and the Rubens " Chapeau de Paille," besides the Hogarths
that I had read of and the Turner " Ulysses and Polyphemus "
that I had seen on a wall in a house where I used to go as a child.
These *Art Journals* had all kinds of miscellaneous information
— pictures from English history like Ward's " James II Hearing
of the Landing of the Prince of Orange," Dr. Johnson in Lord
Chesterfield's waiting room, Hogarth's portrait of Garrick and
his wife, some of Thornbury's scenes from the lives of English
artists, and articles about Nuremberg and Albrecht Dürer, with
Longfellow's " foamy fountains " of St. Sebald's shrine, the
burghers, Hans Sachs and the view of Dürer's grave.

" Emigravit " is the inscription on the tombstone where he lies;
Dead he is not, but departed, for the artist never dies.

This was the beginning of an interest in Dürer and his work
which has grown with the years. In one of my books —
Country Life — there was a story called " The Adventures
of a Pin." At one period of its existence this pin had lived in a
house where the family read aloud, among other books, *The
Heir of Redclyffe*. This made me want to read it, too, and I
found in it allusions to La Motte Fouqué's *Sintram*. I soon
discovered that it was founded upon the idea of Dürer's Knight
riding on undismayed by Death or the Devil, and it was a great
pleasure to renew and extend my acquaintance with him
through some of the woodcuts, and later through a book of
his drawings and color sketches in the British Museum. It was,
I think, my interest in the stage, in Garrick and Mrs. Siddons,
and in Ward's pictures that led me to a somewhat intimate

acquaintance with eighteenth-century London, its men of letters and the actors who made it famous.

Charles Reade's *Art, a Dramatic Tale*, which Ellen Terry made familiar to American playgoers as *Nance Oldfield*, was at that time published in weekly installments in the *Liberator*, an Abolition paper, and I remember the vivid picture of the eighteenth-century stage and the " Rival Queens," Roxana and Statira, acted by Mrs. Bracegirdle and Mrs. Oldfield.

I can date my first reading of a novel by the place where I read it. When the little sister, seven and a half years to a day younger than I, was a few weeks old I was left with her and my mother, with instructions to call someone if they needed anything. As an inducement to be very quiet *The Lamplighter*, then new, was given me to read. The woes of little Gerty, her years in the old part of Boston when the kind lamplighter took her home, her life with the Grahams after his death, her journey up the Hudson, her heroic conduct and the romantic ending to the tale made a deep impression on me.

It was in the summer of the same year that I fell down a steep flight of stairs and, as a consolation for aches and bruises, was offered *Uncle Tom's Cabin*. I read it so many times that when I later heard Mrs. Stowe's son tell " How Uncle Tom's Cabin was Built," repeating some of the scenes almost literally, I found so many of the phrases familiar and like household words that I could have helped him if his memory had failed and told many things that he omitted. I could have described the cake that Aunt Chloe invited George to share, the difficulties thrown in the way of Haley starting in pursuit of Eliza, the scene at the senator's and in the Quaker family and just how Cassy and Emmeline's hiding place in Legree's garret was made and furnished.

About this time I began to go to school. My mother had taught me to read and write and spell, besides a little arithmetic and geography, but with four children she had her hands full. So my brother and I were sent to a small, private school in a large, low, sunny room of an old-fashioned house, up whose yard we could go at recess to a blacksmith's shop and watch him shoeing horses — a never-failing pleasure. I can smell my school reader now! There was an odor about the printer's ink that always remained in it. It was *The Gradual Reader* with which I was already familiar in the older edition that my mother had used at school. Hers ended soon after " Thomas and his Little Sister," but it included the little girl with whom I have always had the deepest sympathy — " The Bad Seamstress." Our friends Rollo and Lucy were in the book and " Self Denial ":

" I should like another, I think, mother," said Frank, just as he had dispatched a large hemisphere of mince pie.

"Any more for you, my dear Harry? " said his mother.

" If you please. No, thank you, though," said Harry, withdrawing his plate. " For," thought he, " I have had enough and more than enough to satisfy my hunger, and now is the time for self-denial."

One of the poems, " The Pretended Morning Drive," was by Mary Howitt and a great favorite. I have found it recently in Mrs. Forbes' *Favorites of a Nursery of Seventy Years Ago*. Others were less cheerful. " The Little Graves," for instance, and

I like it not — this noisy street,
I never liked, nor can I now.

In the additions to the later edition was:

> There once was a man who contrived a balloon
> To carry him whither? Why, up to the moon.

And years and years afterward when I climbed up from Salisbury to see where Old Sarum once had been, it was not on account of Sidney Smith's famous Rotten Borough article, but for the sake of the milestone:

> Twelve miles to Old Sarum,
> To Andover, nine

that undeceived the man when he thought he was in the moon.

After *The Gradual Reader* had been read through, the next step was to Swan's *Grammar School Reader*. Up to that time I had not known much about poetry, barring *Mother Goose* and other infantile jingles, the poems in *The Gradual Reader* and Mrs. Turner's "Daisy" and "Cowslip" verses in reprint; but this book opened a new world. Here was "The Deserted Village," "The Pet Lamb," "The Butterfly's Ball," "The Winged Worshippers," "The Shepherd and the Philosopher," "The Needless Alarm," "Extracts from Beattie and Byron," Wordsworth's "Fidelity" and the poem that made the deepest impression of all, with long lines, solemn diction, and a wonderful choice of words — Gray's "Elegy in a Country Churchyard," whose opening stanzas I remember learning for the love of the sound of them. The story of "Eyes and No Eyes," too, appealed to a dawning sense of out-of-door beauty, and "The Boy without a Genius," "Alexander and the Robber" and "Charles the Second and William Penn" have never been forgotten.

I have spoken of Wordsworth's "Fidelity." Somewhere,

somehow I had found and liked better Scott's version of the same tale, "Helvellyn." It may have been in *Youatt on the Dog* or *The Dog and the Sportsman* — from which I learned every breed and every disease of dogs — but I think that I first saw it in Anna Cabot Lowell's *Gleanings from the Poets*. The melody of it always haunted me. When later on I heard an Englishman answer "Catchedicam" to the question, "What is that mountain?" that we saw from Dunmail Raise, and an American girl say quickly, "He is making fun of us, he made up that queer name," I knew that she had never read over and over:

But meeter for thee, gentle lover of Nature,
To lay down thy head like the meek mountain lamb;
When, wildered, he drops from some cliff huge in stature,
And draws his last sob by the side of his dam;
And more stately thy couch by the desert lake lying,
Thy obsequies seen by the gray plover flying,
With one faithful friend but to witness thy dying
In the arms of Helvellyn and Catchedicam.

The book had been passed on to Jenny by an older sister, who being a Young Lady and going to Evening Parties, had no more use for school books. I used to borrow it when lessons were done to find a poem to repeat or to lose myself in the pages. They had a wide range, from "Busy, curious, thirsty fly" to "The Ancient Mariner." The poem that I loved best was Lockhart's "Lamentation for Celin." I cannot look at the book now without seeing the mournful procession at the Vega Gate and hearing the slow tread of the horses, the wailing of the black-veiled sisters, the beat of the muffled drums, the shriek of the old nurse, all lamenting for "Granada's darling knight," lying dead with black crusted blood on his armor.

We had some dearly loved books that some older cousins had outgrown, books of the early forties. Among them was *The Crofton Boys, Masterman Ready* and *The Fairy Cabinet* — a little book bound in blue, translated from some of the " Cabinet de Fées." It had " The Blue Bird " and " Finetta Cindretta." The two lines that the Princess says to the bird,

> Blue Bird, thou of Time's own hue,
> Haste thee to thy mistress true,

are in no other edition. There were, too, some volumes of *Parley's Magazine*, with Miss Leslie's *Week of Idleness* and stories of the boyhood of noted men. Knowing *The Crofton Boys* it was a great pleasure, long years afterward, to look out of the upper windows of a hotel just off Fleet Street and see " the leads " and watch the steamers going by on the Thames. One of the cousins' books was, as I remembered it, a volume of *Coleman's Magazine*, but I tried in vain to find it under that title in the Boston Public Library. In it were Tennyson's " May Queen," " Piping down the Valleys Wild " and Hunt's "Abou Ben Adhem." There were riddles, too, and puzzles, Hawthorne's " Daffy-down-Dilly " and some other good stories. I did not get a copy of it until one Christmas, when a children's librarian several hundred miles away, who knew nothing of my search for the magazine, sent me a package of old books that she could not use and among them was my old friend, bound under the title *The Boys' and Girls' Annual*.

A school reader with a green cover and a sheepskin back came also from the cousins. I do not remember the title nor the name of the compiler, but I do recall that in it I made acquaintance with three famous poems — "John Gilpin," "The Battle of Blenheim" and "The Cataract of Lodore." What a "trainband captain eke" was I did not know, nor did I ask, for I had a way of keeping to myself whatever puzzled me, but Cheapside and Islington were two more of the places which I must see in London, and I had firm faith that Lodore was always doing everything that Southey said. Fortunately this faith has never been disturbed, for, instead of trickling over bare rocks as some travelers have described it, the cataract when I saw it was behaving even better than in the photographs, pouring masses of white foam into Derwentwater.

Not far from the slave seats in the gallery corner of the old, square, white, slender-steepled church where Theodore Parker had preached for several years in the days when some of the Brook Farm used to listen to him every Sunday, there was a bookcase which must have held two or three hundred volumes, the library for the Sunday School, which was open on Sunday mornings every year from May to November, not in winter from the difficulty of heating the church in the early mornings. There were in it, as far as I can remember, no memoirs of children who died young — indeed I never saw one until after I grew up. My especial favorites there were two fat volumes, *Howitt's Tales* and *Howitt's Stories*, in one of which the heroine had for tea "hot pikelets," which I afterward found in Derbyshire. Another, "Little Coin, Much Care," was more real than ever when I saw the half-burned ruins of Nottingham Castle. The best of all was "Strive and Thrive," the story of a widow and her children who kept a little shop in London. The daughter, who had learned to make designs for wall-paper, had one of the designs stolen and later identified by a mouse peeping from behind an acanthus leaf that she had sketched in the British Museum.

In our village street was a large house where two sisters used to live, in an atmosphere of old-fashioned elegance. Going into the hall, with its crimson-carpeted winter parlor on the south, its blazing fire with the ladies sitting before it with little screens to shield their faces, was like walking into a book. So was the entrance in summer into the north parlor, cool and dark, with a green, mossy carpet and the portrait of the Beautiful Lady in low-necked, crimson velvet dress and gauzy scarf, with her hand on a stair rail. She kept her beauty, even when her hair was white, and with it her love of books. Her room upstairs was fairly crammed with them, and a bookseller in town had a standing order to send her whatever was best worth reading. She was very generous, too, in lending and in giving to her friends. I have several books of later years with her name in them, that she passed on to me. One day she lent me a volume, not new, that she thought would please a bookish little girl. It was the first edition of Drake's poems with " The Culprit Fay," which I read with great delight. The music of the verse, the descriptions and the fairy tale all combined into a new and charming whole. At another time she gave me Henrik Hertz's *King Rene's Daughter*, a romantic little play of much sweetness which has been a rôle to more than one great actress and is still a favorite with amateurs, a play entirely innocent and idyllic.

One day I found in our attic a shabby old copy of *Pickwick* in two volumes. I read it, then *David Copperfield*, which I have yet, incomplete and with covers dropping off after being read many times by every member of the family. *The Christmas Carol* was read in school once by one of the

MR. PEG

From " Carl Krinken: His Christmas Stocking "
by Susan and Anna Warner

teachers as a consolation for a hoped-for half holiday that
was not granted. Not long after, the Beautiful Lady lent it to
me in the first edition with colored plates.

I got my first idea of an English dramatic performance, the
Christmas mumming play, from the Warner Sisters, whose

novels and, later, children's books, are crammed with theology and sickly sentiment. Their *Mr. Rutherford's Children* is full of an old-fashioned fragrance and shows the happy, well-ordered life of two little sisters in their uncle's country house. In *Carl Krinken and His Christmas Stocking* every one of the simple presents given by a poor fisherman's wife to her little boy tells its own story to him. The stocking itself describes a Christmas Eve in an old English manor-house, where the village mummers act the St. George play, with the words quoted nearly in full, much like Mrs. Ewing's *Peace Egg*, which I have used for a Settlement Christmas play. I am sure that I should never have thought of acting it if it had not been for the scene I used to love to read over and over, the entrance of the mummers before the old Squire and his family, and the valiant Saint who

Fought the fiery dragon and brought him to the slaughter,
And saved a beauteous Princess and a King of England's daughter.

In the thirties and forties, among many annuals for grown-up readers, were a few for children. In an odd volume of *The Annualette*, one of the cousins' books, was a colored frontispiece of the Arctic bluebird, and the opening poem was Alexander Wilson's "Bluebird." The descriptive touches in it are those of a keen observer and a nature lover:

When Winter's cold tempests and snows are no more,
Green meadows and brown furrowed fields reappearing,
The fishermen hauling their shad to the shore,
And cloud-cleaving geese to the lakes fast are steering.

When first the lone butterfly flits on the wing,
When red grow the maples, so fresh and so pleasing,

Oh, then comes the bluebird, the herald of Spring,
And hails with his warblings the charms of the season;

Then loud-piping frogs make the marshes to ring,
Then warm glows the sunshine and fine is the weather;
The blue woodland flowers just beginning to spring,
And spicewood and sassafras budding together.

Nature study was not in my school course, but I loved, and still love, the poem because I had been taught at home to watch for the first bluebird, to search for the first " blue woodland flowers " and to listen for the first peeping hylas and the honk of the wild geese.

The Annualette was made up, for the most part, of translations from the French and German, the stories borrowed from Mary Russell Mitford, Mrs. S. C. Hall or Mary Howitt; but this poem had a distinctly American, even New England, note.

A few grown-up annuals in the house were read over and over again. One was an odd volume of *The Token*, edited by S. G. Goodrich (Peter Parley) under his own name, with contributions signed by Mrs. Sigourney, Grenville Mellen, Miss Sedgwick and other names familiar to readers of magazines of the thirties. There was another even more delightful than this — *Friendship's Offering* for 1835. It was in the English edition with really charming " embellishments," a group called " Childhood " by Chalon, of a mother and her three little girls with a poem by Mary Howitt and, best of all, " The Brazilian Bride " to illustrate a highly sentimental and improbable tale by Mrs. Norton. The poem that makes the book valuable to collectors is " Salzburg," signed J. R., a poem whose subject, illustration and signature meant nothing to me until I recognized it not many years ago in a volume of Ruskin's collected poems. He was sixteen when he wrote this and two others, "Andernach" and " St. Goar," published without illustrations in the same annual.

Harper's Magazine had been coming every month ever since I had begun to read. Abbott's Napoleon (one of the children used to ask, " Why did Josephine always call him ' mona mi ' ? " pronounced as in the counting-out game) and Louis XIV, who was, to me, to be envied because he always had a roast chicken by his bedside in case he should wake and feel hungry in the night, were entertaining and full of pictures. Thomson's Seasons were less amusing but quite as pictorial. The magazines had, besides, all kinds of miscellaneous articles, historical, descriptive, biographical, from church festivals in Brazil to Benjamin Franklin walking the streets of Philadelphia with a roll under each arm. There were stories, too — a ghostly legend about one of the kings of Sweden that haunts me yet — Miss Manning's Household of Sir Thomas More, a stray chapter or two of Cranford about the visit to Thomas Holbrook and his quotations from Tennyson and — think of it! — Bleak House, The Newcomes and Little Dorrit coming out in numbers! Imagine reading them in a child's way — the way of a child who has never yet got over the habit of skipping, but who gained an intimate acquaintance with the house of low ceilings and staircases with queer turnings, the kind, elderly guardian who made it a pleasant home for three young folks, with round-eyed Charley and the Smallweeds, the Jellybys and the Turveydrops and the Old Girl's birthday. Is there a better opening for a child into the world of music and art than that chapter in The Newcomes where Miss Cann plays on the old, cracked piano and the sickly, almost deformed J. J. translates the sounds into forms, knights in armor, splendid young noblemen, banditti and lovely maidens?

It was to *Harper's Magazine* that most of the Americans of that day owed their knowledge of John Leech, his hunting sketches, his pretty English girls, his mustache-growing boy or whiskered young officers, his Frenchmen and his dogs. For every month for several years, just before the fashions at the end, there were two pages of " Selections from Punch," an inestimable gift to readers in the United States. What a joy it was to find in my grown-up years a friend who had kept the old, bound volumes, and knew by heart the Leech pictures, the stories in The Editor's Drawer and Porte Crayon's " Virginia Illustrated."

My first knowledge of Washington Irving was through the Darley outline illustrations to *Sleepy Hollow*, with all their humor and life, and perhaps through an extract from *The History of New York* in one of the readers. One day there was a thunder shower, and as I did not enjoy being kept in a room with shut windows and preferred standing at an open door, I was beguiled into forgetfulness of heat and lack of oxygen by the offer of Irving from the grown-up bookcase. It was the double-columned volume that opened *The Alhambra*, the gate with the hand holding the key, the magic tower, the mimic battle, the Arabian astrologer and the Christian maiden down, down in the caverns. It opened, too, the touching, tender story of " The Rose of the Alhambra " and " The Lady of the Fountain," the journey of the Rose to the same cavern and the tale of " The Three Princesses." I never stopped to ask if the words were long or the style was prolix, but read, read, read until the sky was clear and the sun shone. I had found a treasure, and I went on to *Bracebridge Hall*, the Old Christmas chapters in *The Sketch Book* and *The Tales of* a *Traveller.* Even the gruesome story about the student and the guillotine was a mine of fearful pleasure, only equaled by "William and Helen," Scott's translation of Burger's *Lenore* and his *Frederick and Alice,* with their ghosts, skeletons and demons. I was not yet ready for Scott's long poems, but I had, I think, read "The Bridal of Triermain," and I know that I loved one of the dramas which nobody reads nowadays — "The Doom of Devorgoil," with its adaptation of the tale of the ghostly barber in Musaeus' "Dumb Love," that I have told to children at Hallowe'en.

Under the eaves of our house was a large box covered with wall-paper and full of old magazines. *Godey's* and *Graham's* and the three numbers, all that were ever published, of Lowell's *Pioneer.* What ghastly stories by Hawthorne and Poe, "The Telltale Heart," "The Birthmark," "The Oblong Box," "Thou Art the Man" were in those odd numbers! There were milder tales, too, by Eliza Leslie, sister of Charles Leslie, the artist, who made use of her early life in England in a tale called "The Manderfields," the experience of an American family in London not long after the Revolution. It described an amusing evening spent by the children at a party given by their landlady, where her other guests were the valets and maids of great personages. It was not all a high-life-below-stairs atmosphere in which the children lived, for they made another friend in the Park, an American who had taken the King's side in the Revolution and was an exile. Another of Miss Leslie's entertaining stories was of an Englishman, a blustering, self-styled patriot, who with his family and a so-called Countess, said to have received her title from Prince Charlie's widow, the Countess of Albany, quartered themselves for months upon a hospitable American family, and were at last induced to make a moonlight flitting by a hired man who caused them to believe that the house was an Inn, and that their host was on the point of sending them a large bill for board and lodging.

Another story, " The Centre Table," has half a dozen reminiscences that are valuable as studies of social life in Philadelphia from 1800 to 1840. There is a ball, a children's party about 1800 and a young housekeeper's trials. The most tantalizing of Miss Leslie's tales was "Amelia, or a Young Lady's Vicissitudes," because the first numbers were missing and I never read them until a few years ago when our library came into possession of a set of Godey. Amelia was the daughter of an innkeeper of German descent in what, a hundred years ago, was the West — Ohio or Pennsylvania. She was adopted by a childless couple who died suddenly without providing for her. She had received the usual education of a rich man's daughter in the thirties, and did not know what to do to support herself. Her father, hearing of her forlorn situation, sent her brother to take her home, where she was very wretched on account of the vulgarity and greed of the family and their attitude toward her adopted parents. The brother, the only other member of the family who had good instincts or manners, was in business in another town, and when his employer's wife and daughters invited Amelia to visit them, her sister accepted the invitation, because she was older, and made herself heartily disliked. Of course the story ended well, like most stories in those days. And, even though one swain left Amelia when she was no longer a supposed heiress, another who had long loved her took his place.

Old-fashioned and stilted as the stories are, they have a certain descriptive and satirical power. A note which I have in Miss Leslie's spidery handwriting gives a good idea of her character:

Miss Leslie hopes to complete the article for Mr. Graham by next Tuesday afternoon, when he will please to send for it at five o'clock. It will probably occupy six or seven pages of the Magazine (perhaps not quite so much) but it will be well to have sufficient space reserved.

Miss Leslie thinks it best that she should not be announced as positively a monthly contributor, in case she should not be able to finish articles regularly. It will be well that the public shall understand that all the sketches she writes for the Lady and Gentleman's Magazines are reminiscences of real facts, without any mixture of fiction.

A portrait of Miss Leslie in *Godey's*, with smoothly banded hair, a bonnet trimmed with lilies of the valley and a portfolio labeled " Sketches " is the typical "Authoress " of the forties.

Some of the old Harper two-columned, red-brown, paper-covered novels were in our attic. A very modern woman who had just read *Jane Eyre* for the first time described it to me as the tamest novel she had ever read. She should have read it as one of my school friends did, by a dim lamp when she was alone in the house, or as I did in the attic with the rain pouring on the roof.

Novels of another kind in the box were Frederika Bremer's *Home, Neighbors* and *The President's Daughters*. The first was within a child's comprehension, the different types of character in a family coming within the range of one's own experience and observation — domestic Louise, sunny Eva and the others. But best loved of all was Petrea with her large nose, her awkwardness and her literary ambitions. One strong bond of sympathy with one of the friends of my later years has always been that we both knew by heart Petrea's story of Annette and Belis, who finally surmounted all obstacles to their love, were married, lived henceforth in a cottage surrounded with roses and had eight children in one year, and that Louise's " water-gruel " gown had passed into the family speech and was used to describe any garment of pale or trying color. Another mid-century book that will hold its place is *John Halifax*, which I read during a six weeks' quarantine and remember with great pleasure.

All the school children nowadays know something of Longfellow, even if it is only " Paul Revere's Ride," " The Children's Hour " or *The Hiawatha Primer*. When *Hiawatha* was published, as I needs must look into every new book that came into the house, I opened and read it. *Evangeline* and *The Building of the Ship* were also in the bookcase, and I read them at about the same time. A little later I got a great deal of pleasure out of Longfellow's two prose romances, one of which — *Kavanagh* — has all the fun that was in the poet, reminiscences of schoolboy pranks, of Portland as it was in his childhood, and extracts from his desultory and varied reading. His *Hyperion* gave me an outlook on German poetry and romance. I had read a few of the translations in *Gleanings from the Poets*, but " The Black Knight," the student songs, the merry Heidelberg University life, the glimpses of Bettina Brentano, " The Boy's Wonder Horn " and " The Golden Jar " all excited in me a desire to learn German and see Germany and the Rhine.

A very different book that I loved was Horace and James Smith's *Rejected Addresses*, which no one reads nowadays. It had delicious parodies on the poets of 1810 to 1830 in the form of addresses for the opening of the Drury Lane, — Wordsworth, Scott, Southey, Bryon, Coleridge very cleverly imitated, and some verses of pure, rollicking nonsense or burlesque, like

"The Stranger," which I was to remember a little later when I read *Pendennis*.

At this time a new edition of the Waverley Novels was coming out, two volumes a month, and I remember the growth of the collection in the bookcase. I was told that I might read the stories — an empty form, for I used to read everything that interested me without regard to permission. At first the long, uneventful opening to *Waverley* did not look attractive; but an extract from the end, the execution of Fergus MacIvor, that I found in the *American First Class Book*, led me to read the whole. I was drawn to *Ivanhoe* by a picture in one of the old Annuals and a dimly remembered story in another wherein Rowena's sea-green kirtle and Rebecca's "simarre" appeared at a fancy ball.

After the spell was once upon me, I read every one of the novels, some of them many times over before I was fifteen. The Lowland Scotch, which I had learned from Burns, made the Scotch stories easy. The long poems, as I have said, I did not read until I knew many of the shorter ones and some of the novels. As a child I went to the old-fashioned grammar schoolhouse in the town for a few months, and the first noon-tide that I spent there I found in the school library the beginning of *The Lay of the Last Minstrel*, and read the rest at home with great delight. I did not know *The Lady of the Lake* until I had seen an illustrated copy at a neighbor's house, although the poem had been on our bookshelves all the time. I remember that I made out the old English of *Sir Tristram* in our edition without much trouble, and that Tristan and Isolde were old acquaintances when the Wagner operas began to be the fashion.

Mrs. Jameson's *Poetry of Sacred and Legendary Art*, *Legends of the Madonna* and *Legends of the Monastic Orders* came into the house at about the same time as the Waverley Novels and, though they were early editions in the original pale blue cloth with palms and crowns on the covers, we were always permitted to read them, and got a good deal from them — the lives and legends of the saints which have made all Christian art and symbolism full of story and meaning.

Ackermann's Repository published extracts from the Waverley Novels. The stories in it were neither better nor worse than in other magazines of that period; but it gave me not only the graceful, well-drawn fashion plates of the time, but color prints of Italy and Switzerland, and some of Rowlandson's drawings for *Dr. Syntax* and *Sentimental Travels in the South of France* that taught me to recognize his style. The deaths of George III, Queen Charlotte and the Princess Charlotte within two years caused the publication of a ghastly picture of the Royal Vault at Windsor, with all the coffins on shelves. Most of the fashion plates then were of court mourning. More cheerful pictures were of the celebrated Vienna pack of cards, now found in collections, with a story running through them, and of a " hobbyhorse," the forerunner of the bicycle.

I began to read the *Atlantic* with the first number. The stories that led me out farthest into literature and history were Harriet Prescott Spofford's, with their sumptuous style and their allusions to poetry and drama, and Rose Terry Cooke's " Sphinx's Children " and " Metempsychosis." There was no English course in our high school, but the *Atlantic* taught me the use, correct, and incorrect, of many words.

At fifteen I had what it is possible for every child who lives in a town where there is a public library to have, an intimate acquaintance with Dickens, Scott and Irving, some of Thackeray's novels, some Longfellow and Tennyson and Shakespeare's comedies. Some chance words spoken by the teacher with whom we were studying Voltaire's *Siècle de Louis XIV* set us to reading Macaulay's history, and gave us a good working knowledge of the England of 1700.

Good magazines for boys and girls began in the sixties. The first was *Our Young Folks*, published by Ticknor and Fields and edited by Lucy Larcom, assisted by John G. Whittier and J. T. Trowbridge. Harriet Beecher Stowe wrote the opening story, " Hum, the Son of Buz," an account of a humming bird that strayed into her conservatory in the rain one day, apparently near dying. It recovered with good care, made itself entirely at home, and lived there for several weeks, taking short flights and coming back, until one day it appeared exhausted and died. Then there was the *Riverside Magazine*, edited by Horace Scudder, and remarkable for its good pictures and interesting stories. It published several of the *Bodley Books*. In one of the early volumes Lucretia Hale told of " The Lady who put Salt in her Coffee" and introduced the Lady from Philadelphia. Mrs. Adeline Whitney wrote " Leslie Goldthwaite" for *Our Young Folks* and followed it with " We Girls." Some of Edward Lear's nonsense poems and some deliciously funny stories by Dickens were in the later volumes.

The influence of books that I read over and over between the ages of five and fifteen has been so great upon my later life, its tastes and pursuits, that in the last twenty years I have collected copies of as many of them as possible for a standard of comparison with what children read now. They have come from second-hand bookshops, from attics, from booksellers' catalogues and from friends breaking up housekeeping and as careful to find a good home for every old book as if it were a cherished cat. Some of my own have always been in my possession.

Others that had been given to a Sunday school library were brought back after they had been damaged by fire; I promised a new volume for every old one found.

The collection, small at first, began to grow, thanks to three second-hand book dealers near by, and to lists from other cities. It is not an antiquary's library, for there are only a few books in it of earlier date than 1800, and the most expensive one that I ever bought was a little more than five dollars. Once in a bookseller's window I saw some old friends brought from the basement and offered for sale at five cents each. They included Tom Thumb, Dame Hecket and an instructive Jack Horner telling the sources of the " ingredients chief," like " sugar and beef," the " currants all black from the Island of Zante " and " the many nice things of which his mince pie was made." It is hardly necessary for me to say that I bought a copy of every one that I could remember, and one or two more for good measure.

It is not easy to find colored picture books in good repair, but they sometimes come unexpectedly to a collector from attics of city houses which are to be pulled down to make room for business blocks, or from carefully preserved relics of some country childhood. No one excepting a collector knows the rich and interesting " finds " in country houses where several generations of a family have lived; but they are not always willing to show their hoards, or — if they do exhibit them — they ask fabulously large prices. Many of my old-fashioned books have been given me. Nearly a hundred years ago a motherless little girl was sent from Philadelphia to school in Hartford, where she stayed until she was married. Her father used to send her books, usually tales with a moral, illustrated by steel engravings. They were kept by her descendants until they built a house a little out of town, when they gave them to me. They are interesting, because early in the last century Philadelphia issued more books for children than any other city, and Mary kept hers in excellent condition.

Richard Hengist Horne, a friend of Elizabeth Browning and author of an almost forgotten poem called " Orion," wrote for children under the name of Mrs. Fairstar — *The Memoirs of a London Doll* and *The Doll and Her Friends* told by the doll herself in a charmingly simple and natural manner. The descriptions of the toymaker's attic, the confectioner's shop with the Twelfth-cakes, little Ellen's hard life at the milliner's, the doll's change of residence, the London Parks and the Christmas Pantomime all aided in making London as real to me as Boston. Mr. Horne wrote another book at about the same time, called *The Good-Natured Bear*, which I wished very much to read, but never saw until I grew up. Then I found it among some books that a friend of mine had kept from her childhood. It was years later when I was asked in a bookshop to go into the basement to see some interesting books that were for sale. Almost the first one that I saw was *The Good-Natured Bear!* I did not scream for joy, but I said something that made the salesman ask if I had seen a mouse! I said no, but that I had found a book that I had been hoping for years to own. It had come from the library of James T. Fields, and was and is in excellent condition.

PETER PIPER'S
ALPHABET

PETER PIPER'S
ALPHABET

THE FOLLOWING ALPHABET
IS REPRODUCED FROM
PETER PIPER'S PRACTICAL PRINCIPLES
OF PLAIN AND PERFECT
PRONUNCIATION

"Peter Piper" was first published in America about 1830 by Carter Andrews and Company, Lancaster, Massachusetts. We are indebted to the Lancaster Town Library for permission to reproduce the quaint woodcuts used in that early edition. It is interesting to note that in the cut on the preceding page (representing "Francis Fribble on a Frenchman's Filly") appears a milestone marked "Bolton (a neighboring town to Lancaster) 4 M," adding a local New England touch to these originally English jingles.

A a

ANDREW AIRPUMP ask'd his Aunt her Ailment:
Did Andrew Airpump ask his Aunt her Ailment?
If Andrew Airpump ask'd his Aunt her Ailment,
Where was the Ailment of Andrew Airpump's Aunt?

Billy Button bought a butter'd Biscuit:
Did Billy Button buy a butter'd Biscuit?
If Billy Button bought a butter'd Biscuit,
Where's the butter'd Biscuit Billy Button bought?

Captain Crackskull crack'd a Catchpoll's Cockscomb:
Did Captain Crackskull crack a Catchpoll's Cockscomb?
If Captain Crackskull crack'd a Catchpoll's Cockscomb,
Where's the Catchpoll's Cockscomb Captain Crackskull
    crack'd?

D d

Davy Dolldrum dream'd he drove a Dragon:
Did Davy Dolldrum dream he drove a Dragon?
If Davy Dolldrum dream'd he drove a Dragon,
Where's the Dragon Davy Dolldrum dream'd he drove?

Enoch Elkrig ate an empty Eggshell:
Did Enoch Elkrig eat an empty Eggshell?
If Enoch Elkrig ate an empty Eggshell,
Where's the empty Eggshell Enoch Elkrig ate?

F f

Francis Fribble figured on a Frenchman's Filly:
Did Francis Fribble figure on a Frenchman's Filly?
If Francis Fribble figured on a Frenchman's Filly,
Where's the Frenchman's Filly Francis Fribble figur'd
        on?

Gaffer Gilpin got a Goose and Gander:
Did Gaffer Gilpin get a Goose and Gander?
If Gaffer Gilpin got a Goose and Gander,
Where's the Goose and Gander Gaffer Gilpin got?

H h

Humphrey Hunchback had a Hundred Hedgehogs:
Did Humphrey Hunchback have a Hundred Hedge-
    hogs?
If Humphrey Hunchback had a Hundred Hedgehogs,
Where's the Hundred Hedgehogs Humphrey Hunch-
    back had?

Inigo Impey itched for an Indian Image:
Did Inigo Impey itch for an Indian Image?
If Inigo Impey itch'd for an Indian Image,
Where's the Indian Image Inigo Impey itch'd for?

Jumping Jacky jeer'd a jesting Juggler:
Did Jumping Jacky jeer a jesting Juggler?
If Jumping Jacky jeer'd a jesting Juggler,
Where's the jesting Juggler Jumping Jacky jeered?

Kimbo Kemble kick'd his Kinsman's Kettle:
Did Kimbo Kemble kick his Kinsman's Kettle?
If Kimbo Kemble kick'd his Kinsman's Kettle,
Where's the Kinsman's Kettle Kimbo Kemble kicked?

Lanky Lawrence lost his Lass and Lobster:
Did Lanky Lawrence lose his Lass and Lobster?
If Lanky Lawrence lost his Lass and Lobster,
Where are the Lass and Lobster Lanky Lawrence lost?

Matthew Mendlegs miss'd a mangled Monkey:
Did Matthew Mendlegs miss a mangled Monkey?
If Matthew Mendlegs miss'd a mangled Monkey,
Where's the mangled Monkey Matthew Mendlegs
    miss'd?

Neddy Noodle nipp'd his Neighbour's Nutmegs:
Did Neddy Noodle nip his Neighbour's Nutmegs?
If Neddy Noodle nipp'd his Neighbour's Nutmegs,
Where are the Neighbour's Nutmegs Neddy Noodle
    nipp'd?

Oliver Oglethorpe ogled an Owl and Oyster:
Did Oliver Oglethorpe ogle an Owl and Oyster?
If Oliver Oglethorpe ogled an Owl and Oyster,
Where are the Owl and Oyster Oliver Oglethorpe
    ogled?

Peter Piper pick'd a Peck of Pepper:
Did Peter Piper pick a Peck of Pepper?
If Peter Piper pick'd a Peck of Pepper,
Where's the Peck of Pepper Peter Piper pick'd?

Quixote Quicksight quiz'd a queerish Quidbox:
Did Quixote Quicksight quiz a queerish Quidbox?
If Quixote Quicksight quiz'd a queerish Quidbox,
Where's the queerish Quidbox Quixote Quicksight
    quiz'd?

Rory Rumpus rode a raw-bon'd Racer:
Did Rory Rumpus ride a raw-bon'd Racer?
If Rory Rumpus rode a raw-bon'd Racer,
Where's the raw-bon'd Racer Rory Rumpus rode?

Sammy Smellie smelt a Smell of Smallcoal:
Did Sammy Smellie smell a Smell of Smallcoal?
If Sammy Smellie smelt a Smell of Smallcoal,
Where's the Smell of Smallcoal Sammy Smellie smelt?

T t

Tip-Toe Tommy turn'd a Turk for Two-pence:
Did Tip-Toe Tommy turn a Turk for Two-pence?
If Tip-toe Tommy turn'd a Turk for Two-pence,
Where's the Turk for Two-pence Tip-Toe Tommy
    turned?

Uncle's Usher urg'd an ugly Urchin:
Did Uncle's Usher urge an ugly Urchin?
If Uncle's Usher urged an ugly Urchin,
Where's the ugly Urchin Uncle's Usher urg'd?

Villiam Veedon vip'd his Vig and Vaistcoat:
Did Villiam Veedon vipe his Vig and Vaistcoat,
If Villiam Veedon vip'd his Vig and Vaistcoat,
Where are the Vig and Vaistcoat Villiam Veedon vip'd?

Walter Waddle won a walking Wager:
Did Walter Waddle win a walking Wager?
If Walter Waddle won a walking Wager,
Where's the walking Wager Walter Waddle won?

X Y Z have made my Brains to crack-o,
X smokes, Y snuffs, and Z chews tobacco;
Yet oft by X Y Z much learning's taught;
But Peter Piper beats them all to nought.

CAROLINE M. HEWINS AND BOOKS FOR CHILDREN

By JENNIE D. LINDQUIST

Caroline reading to her little sister Anna

INTRODUCTION

Did the bright day for library's service to children begin with Caroline Hewins of Hartford? There could be no better figure for the herald of a movement. The characteristics of her methods and service will long be reviewed and retold.

The vigor of Miss Hewins' work and the persistence of her ideals will be preserved by this book, refreshened among those who knew her, and made clear to those of each new generation. Appropriately brought together here are her happy reminiscences of a New England girlhood and Miss Lindquist's warm, sympathetic picture of a busy and useful life.

Miss Hewins was not the meek and wishful lover of children, she lived with and among them healthily and naturally; she was not isolated in the children's department, but saw and felt this service to children as a part of the broad public function of libraries as successful administrator and up-builder of a large city library; she did not use books mechanically as tools for thrusting forward ideas, but books and literature were part of her being and the love of books flowed from her to her community of boys and girls.

It was one of her conceptions of her services to library work with children that there should be carefully winnowed book lists based on intimate knowledge of the children themselves and on a broad and firsthand acquaintance with all the best in the world of literature.

It was in 1882 that she published her famous pamphlet, "Books for the Young," and issued it, it is happy for me to remember, through the office of the Publishers' Weekly. This list extended its influence through a generation and more of librarians and into the thinking of publishing and bookselling and thus to the shelves of home libraries. It was the beginning of a new day in book selection for children, a movement that has never lost its momentum.

In its later revisions, " Books for the Young " was taken over by the American Library Association, and it was in this form that it became my buying guide when I undertook, in the late 90's, to build up the department for children in Lauriat's Boston bookstore. It was a fortunate thing that this wise list fell to my hands, and my growing attention to this sector of the business of books has led to a lifetime interest in the books and reading of boys and girls.

I came to know Miss Hewins later on her visits to Miss Moore and the 42nd Street Room of the New York Public Library. To meet her was to understand the rare personality which makes her story an inspiration to succeeding generations of librarians and to all authors, illustrators and publishers of books for children.

FREDERIC G. MELCHER

The author wishes to thank the members of the Hewins family and all the librarians and other friends who so generously shared their recollections of Miss Hewins.

CAROLINE M. HEWINS
AND BOOKS FOR CHILDREN

By JENNIE D. LINDQUIST

IT WAS soon after the Civil War that Caroline Hewins set out into the world to seek her fortune. She went with the parental blessing, but permission to go had been reluctantly given. In fact, her father was so anxious to keep her at home that he built an ell onto their beautiful house in West Roxbury, with the promise that Caroline should have it for her own if only she would not go away. It is fortunate for Hartford, where for fifty-one years she was the distinguished librarian, and for children's reading throughout the country, that even an ell could not tempt Miss Hewins to give up her plans. Those were the days before library courses were given, but surely no one could have had better preparation for library work — and particularly work with boys and girls — than she had.

She was born October 10, 1846, in Roxbury, Massachusetts. When she was almost two the family moved to Jamaica Plain and later to West Roxbury to a large house and several acres of land that were a great joy to them all. Her father was a lover of gardens, and planted trees, shrubs and flowers. More than a hundred of the trees — fifty-three different varieties — are standing today, and the gardens are still beautiful. For many years the Hewins family gave a Rhododendron Tea on the first Saturday in June so that friends and neighbors might also enjoy the blossoming shrubs and the rest of the garden. One can imagine Caroline playing there through the years with her seven younger sisters and one younger brother. She used to like to startle people by announcing, " There are eight girls in our family and each one has a brother! " Besides Mother and Father, there were living with this lively group a grandmother, two aunts and an uncle. Probably there were pets, too, but I have found mention of only one — a cow named Jessie in 1858 after the " immortal wife " of John Charles Fremont, then a candidate for the presidency.

The house was full of books and Caroline said in later years that she had no recollection of learning to read; it seemed to her that there never was a time when she was unable to read " the words in an ordinary printed book and the marriages, deaths and accidents in the *Boston Evening Transcript.*"

In her own reminiscent volume, *A Mid-Century Child and Her Books*, she wrote:

" I was discovered one Sunday afternoon reading Godey's *Lady's Book* which, although extremely mild and harmless, was thought in those days a little grown-up for a person of four and a half. The next day I was taken into town and made the proud owner of a copy of Jacob Abbott's *Lucy's Conversations*, my first bound book, which I have to this day, with my name and the date in it. It is in this book that Lucy has croup in the night and the next morning is given a powder in jelly and a roasted apple that was cooked by hanging it in front of the fire from a string held by a flat-iron on the mantelpiece."

She was only six when someone gave her *The Man of Snow* by Harriet Myrtle. It became such a favorite that years later she was reading aloud every Christmas to children as well as to adults in Hartford this " record of a joyous Christmas time, when the mother tells little Mary and her two boy cousins about the funny things that happened to a snow man when she was a child."

Another early favorite was Washington Irving's *Alhambra*. She was given a copy of that to look at one day when she had been kept in the house because of a thunder shower; and was immediately captivated. " I never stopped to ask," she says, " if the words were long or the style was prolix, but read, read, read until the sky was clear and the sun shone."

This led her to other books by Irving and before she was fifteen she had an intimate acquaintance with his work; with Dickens and with Scott (always her great favorite); with some of Thackeray's novels; Shakespeare's comedies; Longfellow and Tennyson. She had read *John Halifax Gentleman*, *Jane Eyre*, Frederika Bremer's novels, Macaulay's history and *Mrs. Mowatt's Biography of an Actress*.

The Atlantic and *Harpers* she read from cover to cover and also *The London Art Journals*, which were among the books in the parlor where the family sat on Sunday afternoon.

There were good pictures too in the Hewins household. Caroline's paternal grandfather, Amasa Hewins, was a Boston portrait painter who spent several years in Florence and wrote little Caroline the first letters she ever received. He sent home many treasures, including pictures, for his son Charles, Caroline's father, to sell. Among these treasures still in the possession of the Hewins family is a painting done in Italy by the English nonsense poet, Edward Lear. Charles Hewins went often to England on business, for he was one of the founders of the firm of haberdashers, Hewins and Hollis of Boston. (Although the firm has now been taken over by Filene's, it still bears the original name.)

Both he and his wife loved birds and flowers and imparted

that love to their children. They watched for the first bluebird and for the shadbush that bloomed when the shad came into the rivers. They hunted for the early woodland flowers and listened for the first peeping hylas and the honk of the wild geese. And once, walking by the banks of the Charles River, Caroline came upon a tall bush of pink-purple flowers that she knew, without being told, must be Emerson's " fresh rhodora of the woods."

When she was a very little girl, her mother taught her at home, but as more babies arrived, Caroline and her brother were sent to a private school. In the class above her was another little bookworm, Jenny by name, who " had the run of two libraries, one a minister's, the other the property of a leading Boston publisher." " We came together," Miss Hewins said, " ' like halves of one dissevered world ' and what one had not read the other had, from Miss Yonge's *Daisy Chain* to Edgar Allan Poe."

Caroline did not go to a public school until after she had received her high school diploma. Then she was sent to the Girls' High and Normal School in Boston. She enjoyed the classes and also the social life with girls of her own age. And it is to the principal of this school, Mr. William Seavey, that we owe a vote of thanks, for it was he who decided her future career, although he may have had no idea that he was doing so. He was writing a book and sent her one day to the Boston Athenaeum to do some research for him. She was so much impressed by the scholarly atmosphere of the library that she persuaded her parents to let her go there to work after graduation. Mr. William Frederic Poole, the well-known indexer, was the Athenaeum Librarian, and no doubt it was he who taught her the rudiments and importance of bibliography, so that later when she made her own booklists she did so not only with imagination but also with good style and accuracy.

Although she left the Athenaeum after only one year there, to take some courses at Boston University and to teach in private schools, library work was now in her blood and was never to go out of it.

It was in 1875 that she applied for and got the position of librarian of the Young Men's Institute, a subscription library in Hartford, Connecticut; and her life work really began. The people in Hartford looked askance at her at first and spoke of her as " that woman from Boston," little knowing that fifty years later all Hartford would pay her tribute as its leading citizen.

The population of Hartford in 1875 was about fifty thousand, yet only five or six hundred men and women were subscribers to the Young Men's Institute, paying either three dollars a year for the privilege of taking out one book at a time or five dollars for two. Almost nothing was done for children even in public libraries in those days, but so great was Miss Hewins' interest in boys and girls and their reading that she began at once to think of ways to get more and better books to as many children as possible. It was useless to urge them to join the Young Men's Institute, for only a few families could afford to subscribe. But at least she could begin by examining the book collection to see what there was for those children whose families were members.

Adult and juvenile fiction were shelved together in one alphabet by title. She found that Andersen, Grimm, Hawthorne, Scott, Dickens and Thackeray were on the shelves, but had been read very little compared to books by the authors of whom she always spoke as " the immortal four ": Oliver Optic, Horatio Alger, Harry Castlemon and Martha Finley of Elsie Dinsmore fame. The older girls asked for novels by Ouida, then a new name to Miss Hewins. She took home some of Ouida's books,

Illustration by Margaret Gillies for
" Memoirs of A London Doll "

read them and was not favorably impressed. Immediately she wrote a letter to one of the local newspapers, outlining the plot of a Ouida novel and asking mothers and fathers if they knew what their young daughters were reading. " It [is]," she told them, ". . . a story of today in which are men who have broken every one of the Ten Commandments, and yet are the petted idols of London society. Each of them, having unfortunately married beneath him in early life, and living apart from his wife, makes love in the most sensuously passionate manner to a pure young girl. One of these girls is ready to give up everything for her hero, and is only prevented from leaving her friends and going to him by the opportune death of his wife; and the other, when the first marriage is proved illegal, throws herself into the arms of her ' Sir Folke ' with pretty scriptural phrases and is happy ever after! "

She called in the president of the Young Men's Institute and showed him some of the books by writers for older boys, whose stories were full of profanity and brutal vulgarity. She was given permission to discard these and substituted better books as soon as possible.

For those of us who have done our children's library work in the 1900's it is almost impossible to realize how difficult it must have been to discard and buy wisely in 1875. Good lists of children's books were practically non-existent; and it was in compiling such lists that Miss Hewins made one of her most valuable contributions to the field of children's reading. She had not only read widely by herself; she had also spent many hours reading to her younger brother and sisters and to the children in the private schools where she had taught.

She now urged boys and girls to come into the library, read with them and discussed their likes and dislikes. In 1878, the library began to publish a quarterly bulletin. She saw to it that the first number contained suggestions for good reading for children. Other lists followed in later bulletins.

In 1882, at the request of Frederick Leypoldt, then editor of *Publishers' Weekly*, Miss Hewins compiled *Books for the Young, A Guide for Parents and Children*. It is worth examination. It opens with a preface in Miss Hewins' usual lively style, followed by eight rules for parents on " How to Teach the Right Use of Books." Let me quote from them:

" Do not let them [the children] read anything you have not read yourself.

" Read to them, and teach them to look for the explanation of allusions in books. Do not count time lost in going to the library with them to see a portrait of Queen Elizabeth, or a picture of a Roman chariot, or to find out why mince-pies are eaten at Thanksgiving.

" Do not let them depend on school ' speakers' and the ' Hundred choice selections' for poetry which they must learn. Find it for them in Shakespeare or Scott, or whatever poet you love, and arrange a scene from the ' Midsummer night's dream,' the ' Tempest,' or 'As you like it,' and let them act it at Christmas or on a birthday.

" Remember Jacob Abbott's sensible rule, to give children something that they are growing up to, not away from, and keep down their stock of children's books to the very best."

A section called " English and American History " outlines a reading course of fiction and non-fiction. "A Symposium on Books for Children " includes quotations from a wide variety of sources. Then comes the bibliography itself. It contains lists of home and school stories; of myths, folklore and fairy tales; of historical stories, poetry, and books on nature, science and " counsel and example."

This first edition of *Books for the Young* is a collector's item now and very few people own copies. However, we still have access in most larger libraries to files of *The Library Journal* and *Public Libraries*. The articles Miss Hewins wrote for these magazines cover practically everything upon which our library service for children is built. There are discussions on working with children in the library, in schools and in clubs; on the qualities to be expected in children's librarians; on book reviewing; on the making of lists; and on the possibilities inherent in good reading.

And Miss Hewins was building all this without any pattern to follow. Of course she made mistakes, as she herself acknowledged. All her experience had been with children in her own family and in select private schools, but it was not long before that experience widened.

She persuaded schools to take subscriptions to the Young Men's Institute. Sometimes these were paid for by school funds; sometimes the children themselves raised the money, penny by penny. Thus, collections of books were sent to classrooms where all the children could use them. Mr. Wilbur Gordy, known to most of us through his histories, was principal of the North School. In that capacity and later also as president of the Institute, he worked tirelessly with Miss Hewins, not only for the library but also with boys and girls in the social settlement houses in the city. Naturally he shared her interest in historical stories and together they worked out an arrangement whereby the library provided the schools with such stories and with lists of suggested reading for their American history classes. And when Mr. Gordy took his students on visits to points of historical interest, Miss Hewins always invited them to follow the visits with gingerbread and lemonade in her office.

Dressing the Dragon from " The Peace Egg "
Illustrated by Gordon Browne

[94]

In 1890 she succeeded in having the subscription fee reduced to $1.00 and the membership increased to 1003, the largest in the Institute's history. In 1892 it became a free library and the following year it was officially named the Hartford Public Library.

Although there was still neither space nor funds for a children's room, 50,000 children's books were circulated in the first year of the public library's existence. But it was not enough for Miss Hewins. She continued her work with schools and in 1895 opened a branch in a closet in the North Street Social Settlement House. She became so much impressed with the work going on in the House that she went there to live for twelve years. She read with the children, acted out plays with them and took them for Sunday afternoon nature walks. She followed their activities in school and visited their teachers and their homes.

One Christmas they acted out the ancient Christmas mummers' play about St. George and the dragon, *The Peace-Egg*. Miss Hewins wrote, " I am sure I should never have thought of acting it if it had not been for the scene I used to love to read over and over, the entrance of the mummers before the old Squire and his family, and the valiant Saint who

> Fought the fiery dragon and brought him to the slaughter,
> And saved a beauteous Princess and a King of England's daughter."

It was one of the children at this settlement house who gave me my most vivid picture of Miss Hewins. Miss Annie Fisher, for many years a distinguished principal of a junior high school in Hartford, lived in the North Street neighborhood as a little girl. She recalled that it was Miss Hewins' custom to send to the schools small collections of books for the children to review. Later she herself would come and read aloud the best review. The day she read little Annie Fisher's was a red-letter day for Annie. She recalled, too, an afternoon when she was playing in the street, dressed in " a rather grubby Mother Hubbard." Suddenly Miss Hewins appeared and called, "Annie, want to go to see a garden? " Annie was so excited that she forgot that her dress was dirty and that she should have gone home to tell her mother where she was going. She ran to Miss Hewins' side and went to the garden! It was the first of many happy excursions.

When Annie was twelve she went to work in the library as a page at six cents an hour. One day while Miss Hewins was out at supper Annie finished the work that had been assigned to her. Not knowing what to do next, she took a book and sat down to read while she waited for Miss Hewins to come back. When she did come, an assistant on duty at the desk reported that Annie Fisher had stopped working and spent twenty minutes reading. Annie was called before Miss Hewins. Did she not realize that when she was being paid the time did not belong to her? If she did not understand that clearly, work in the library was not for her. Annie was in despair! That she had wasted two cents which belonged to Hartford might be bad enough; but it was as nothing compared to the awful fact that Miss Hewins thought she had tried to cheat. She was so overwhelmed and hurt that she could never bring herself to explain.

One day Miss Hewins invited Annie to tea in her office. Here were copies of most of the books she had owned in her childhood. Here too were many other books and pictures, as well as treasures from her trips abroad. Here was a tea table with delicate cups and saucers. And *here* was Annie invited to tea! She couldn't say much at the time, but on the way home she could hardly contain herself; she wanted so much to tell her mother all about it. With every step she took the tea party increased in proportions, so that when she dashed up the stairs and told her mother and brother the wonders of it, her brother said, " Now, Annie, if you're going to tell lies, you ought to learn to do it better than that. There couldn't possibly be so many cups and saucers and books and people as you say there were in Miss Hewins' office."

When Miss Hewins found that Annie had never been to the theater she took her to several good plays. She was interested in all her high-school activities, and came to visit her in college. When Annie came back to Hartford to teach, they worked together to increase the use of good books in the schools.

Annie was by no means the only child whose interest Miss Hewins had at heart. Many people who lived in Hartford in those days look back with appreciation of her personal kindness. The following letter which came to me is one of many examples:

" She was one of my idols, when I was a child. . . . She organized an Agassiz Club for young people, and on Saturday mornings took us on long walks to watch for birds and look for wildflowers. I can see her yet, striding along in her tweeds and sensible hat, talking most fascinatingly of things we saw. She never grew impatient and I am sure we must have been enough to try a saint.

" She had a large room on the main floor of the library, fitted up as a study and sitting-room. If she saw a child she knew in the library she would take him or her in for a chat. I can remember that I was fascinated by a bas-relief of Ulysses with his dog. She told me the story of his return after his wanderings, and that only his dog recognized him in his rags. I have never forgotten the story over the years."

In 1896, Miss Hewins met a young woman who was to become to her an inspiration as well as a close personal friend — Anne Carroll Moore. Either alone would have contributed much to the field of children's books; it is impossible to gauge how much their contributions were increased because of the inspiration they gave each other. Miss Moore writes:

" Singularly and, as I think, prophetically of the rare friendship between us, Miss Hewins and I first met in a railway train on the New York, New Haven and Hartford road . . . and across all the years I can still feel the pressure of her friendly hand and the warmth of her welcome to share in everything she had to give on my way to my first A. L. A. in Cleveland. It marked the beginning of all manner of good times at A. L. A.'s, at New York theatres, in Hartford gardens. Wherever and whenever we met, the meeting became a *festa* for both of us."

It was not only when they were together that there was a *festa*. Each had the ability to give that feeling also to others. When I was in library school it was my good fortune to do part of my practice work under Miss Moore at the New York Public Library. I remember how she cast a feeling of festival about everything she did, whether she was receiving one in her office or introducing one to a branch library or to some of her favorite places in New York. So it must have been with Miss Hewins. Those who remember her office from their childhood days and those who knew it as adults all speak of its charm.

Miss Hewins carried the festival spirit with her into the schools and of course into the Settlement House. It must have been one of the things that made all the children there ready at any time to drop whatever they were doing to go adventuring with her.

She loved a party and in one of her letters to Miss Moore she describes a Twelfth Night Frolic at the Settlement House in 1904 for a club of girls called " The Merry Twenty."

" I had the party as much as possible like the old English merry-making. The girls went up into the gymnasium and danced for a while and then a bright college girl and I appeared at the door. She wore a jester's hood of bright scarlet, with bells, and carried a bauble. She was crammed full of conundrums that she fired off in pauses of conversation all the evening. I was the herald, with a trumpet, a tartan of silkoline with large fleur-de-lis and other figures, and a hat to match with two long white feathers. We summoned the company to the banquet in the dining room and the table looked very pretty. Before they went upstairs in the first place, I told them about some Twelfth Night parties I used to go to and somebody — it was Mr. [Edward Everett] Hale, and the parties were at a girls' Orphan Asylum — used to tell the girls that the twelve days of Christmas ought to be the happiest in the year, and the kindest, and I said that if anybody in the Club had any hard feeling toward another, she ought to make it up before the twelve days were over. I happened to know that two of the girls were not on good terms, but do not know whether they took my hint.

" To go back to the table — There was a Twelfth-Cake at each end, with a bean in it; and with holly, red shades, red under the centerpiece, red costumes, crackers, red and green candy, and red bundles of Japanese tapers, the effect was really festive. Some of the crackers had little musical instruments, and the girls were allowed to make all the noise they pleased. They looked very pretty in their caps; and the king and queen were very fetching in gilt paper crowns, trimmed with tinsel filched from the Christmas-tree, and a star in front of the king's. They had sceptres to match. While the girls were eating their cake and ice-cream, they drew cards with names on them like Lord Reginald Rougedragon and Lady Felicia Fitz-Rosemary or Lady Penelope Popocatapetl and then went up to the gymnasium again. The king and queen sat on a throne, and as the Club is the Merry Twenty they decorated the girls who had drawn lords' names with the Order of the Grin, a scarlet sash, and the ladies with the Order of the Giggle. Then they danced and played games, and at last we formed a procession, everyone carrying a lighted Japanese taper, and went through the house to bless it and keep off the evil spirits for the year.

"In the capacity of herald, I gave them a little Herrick before the feast, and the end of A Midsummer Night's Dream while we were going through the house. Every girl had a little gift to take home — a 12½ cent novel, tied up attractively — I don't hold with cheap editions for libraries, but really when you can buy Jane Eyre or The Last Days of Pompeii or A Hardy Norseman or The House of the Seven Gables and give it to a girl who has few or no books at home, it may be the beginning of book-buying for her instead of candy.

"They all had a good time and I am sure that I did."

Although Miss Hewins was now doing more library work for children *without* a children's room than most people do *with* one, she realized that a room was essential. It took a long time and much hard work to convince the city, but finally the last straw broke the resistance — a newspaper picture of the reference room one Sunday afternoon with one man, one woman and fifty-one children in it.

And so in 1904, when the library secured space in an old-fashioned house next door, a children's room was finally opened. Gifts for it poured in from far and wide, for people throughout the country had heard of Miss Hewins' good work — andirons for the open fireplace, a cuckoo clock, some Japanese prints, a Boston fern, a case of native and foreign stuffed birds, several pictures, two trunks of curiosities from all over the world, a check to buy wall decorations, and " a check for unnecessary things."

Now, of course, children's work grew faster than ever. There were interesting exhibits, book talks and story hours. In addition to the Agassiz Club there was now a Puzzle Club to teach the younger children how to do the puzzles in *St. Nicholas* and other magazines. And at last there was a children's librarian, Sarah S. Eddy. But even after her coming, Miss Hewins spent a good deal of time in the room, joining in all the festivities as well as in the daily work with the children. She prepared exhibits of books suggested as Christmas gifts and spent Sunday afternoons in November and December advising parents and friends what books to buy for their boys and girls. She had collected foreign dolls on her trips abroad and every New Year's Day there was a doll story hour, when all the little girls in the city were invited to bring their Christmas dolls to meet the dolls from other countries.

She not only helped the boys and girls put on plays based on their favorite stories but also performed in them herself with the greatest delight and abandon. They acted " Cinderella," " Bluebeard " and " Beauty and the Beast " on the lawn outside the library. One May Day she and Miss Eddy staged an old English festival around a Maypole, to which Miss Hewins wrote the invitation:

> " Next Saturday from out the wood
> In Lincoln green comes Robin Hood,
> Holding Maid Marian by the hand,
> And followed by a valiant band,
> Will Scarlet, lusty Little John,
> With all his woodland finery on.
> ' Little ' though several inches higher
> Than Tuck, the fat and jolly Friar,
> The Fool and Hobby-horse make way
> For Lord and Lady of the May.
> Jack-in-the-green and Milkmaids quail
> Before the Dragon's jaw and tail,

But when the Maypole fast is set,
They all join hands and say, ' Well met! '
Dancing three times around the Queen
Who waits enthroned upon the green.
Say, will you come to keep the May
When thrice the cuckoo sings his lay?
At three the Maypole will be ready.

Yours,

C. M. Hewins
and
S. S. Eddy "

All the characters mentioned in the invitation were there and more besides and the festival was such a success that they were invited to repeat it at East Hartford.

When Miss Hewins was traveling she thought of the children. She sent them letters and postcards, and each week they met in the library and read about and discussed the places she was visiting. Her letters always drew the children into books or reminded them of reading which her descriptions now made more vivid.

" Dear Boys and Girls:" she wrote, " It's no use trying to get away from you and the books! I can't do it, for everywhere I go there is something to make me think of them and you. Before the train was more than an hour out, it passed the signboard about the ' Free Soil Road,' at Clark's Corners, that Nathan Bodley and his cousin saw on their walk from Boston in ' The Bodleys Afoot.' "

She wrote from the Walker Art Gallery in Liverpool: " There are so many pictures taken from stories and plays that the more you have read, the more friends you find in a picture gallery, and in this one, you see Robinson Crusoe and Friday,

Richard Coeur de Lion and Saladin, Don Quixote and Joan of Arc."

From Sicily: " Sicily was . . . Persephone's country, you know, and it is just at this time of year that she comes back and the grass grows green under her returning feet."

And from Algiers: " Cats flourish in the Arab town — tiger, black and white, yellow and other varieties, all sleek and well fed. You remember that the Barbary coast was infested with rats till Dick Whittington sent the pet that made his fortune, and probably some of these are her descendants."

The letters were published in a Hartford newspaper and years later Miss Moore urged Miss Hewins to take them to Louise Seaman at Macmillan's. A selection was made; Miss Hewins chose her favorite pictures of many places and in 1923 *A Traveler's Letters to Boys and Girls* was published. This led to the publication in 1926 of *A Mid-Century Child and Her Books.*

It was not only her own Hartford children and children's room in which Miss Hewins was interested. She visited many others and was eager to help wherever she went. Most of all she loved to visit Miss Moore's room, first at Pratt Institute in Brooklyn and later at the New York Public Library. Whenever she could she went to New York on Hallowe'en to the first story hour of the season and delighted everyone by her recitation of the famous " Peter Piper's Alphabet," which she called her one parlor trick.

She was vitally interested also in the children's libraries which the American Committee for Devastated France established after World War I; and was proud that one of her own Agassiz Club girls, Alice O'Connor, had been put in charge of the work at the center in Soissons. When Miss Moore went to France and visited the libraries, Miss Hewins could scarcely wait to hear her report of the work going on there.

In the midst of marveling at all the things Miss Hewins did for children's books one is suddenly startled to remember that she wasn't a children's librarian. She was the administrator of a busy city library. She was interested in civic affairs and took her place in the adult life of the city. She organized an Education Association that was a forerunner of the P. T. A. Before the Connecticut Public Library Association had a paid worker she, as its secretary, drove a horse and buggy from one small library to another, giving her counsel and help.

She was active in the American Library Association and the Connecticut Library Association from their beginnings. It is a matter of A.L.A. record that she was the first woman to speak from the floor of that assembly. If you think some pearl of great wisdom fell from her lips upon that momentous occasion you may be disappointed. She is reported to have said, " How many libraries use the dog tax to buy books? "

However, many were the pearls of wisdom she contributed through the years at A. L. A. conferences, in more than one branch of library work. As I read the reports of meetings on children's books and reading, where she took an active part in the discussions, I thought, " Why, I've read most of this before and heard it many times." And then I realized that here was Miss Hewins saying it all *first*.

It seems incredible that one woman could accomplish all she did. " How did she do it? " I asked and those who knew her answered, " Well, she was so full of the zest for living; she had such gaiety and such a sense of humor." Her assistant, Miss Alice Cummings, told me that on days when everything went wrong and most people would have been in despair, Miss

Hewins used to quote from a well-loved book, " Oh, dear, oh, dear, was mortal ever so put upon — wife dying upstairs, mad dog down! " And somehow order was restored. Miss Cummings added that she remembered one day Miss Hewins came into the library laughing to herself; when asked what the joke was, she replied that she had met a boy on the library steps who made up a dreadfully saucy face at her. " What did you do? " asked Miss Cummings. " Oh," answered Miss Hewins, " I made up a *much* worse face at him! "

Her good friend, Mrs. Mary Root, also spoke of Miss Hewins' sense of humor and her ability to make a gay occasion out of even a trivial happening. She told me about the dog who arrived at the library, made himself at home and of course had to have a name. Trust Miss Hewins to find an original way of providing it. To quote Mrs. Root:

" The ceremony of naming his dogship was a function of state. Choice canine foods were offered on individual platters. Each platter was named and the name on the platter which was His Majesty's choice was to be his name. He chose, ' Moreover, the dogs,' of Biblical allusion, afterward shortened to ' Moro.' His favorite watch-post was the window facing on Main Street where he could pass judgment on ingoing and outgoing library patrons. When they proved too boring he would rush out, jump on a passing trolley, ride to the terminal and back, refreshed, to his customary duties."

Years ago I called on two of Miss Hewins' sisters and one of them said to me, " Caroline was the most cheerful person I have ever known. She never could abide gloom. If it seemed to threaten us she would think of something exciting for us to do to dispel it and we'd soon be having fun again. To the time of her death she was ready for adventure any time, with children or grown-ups. She was interested in everything and everybody."

It is no wonder that Hartford people forgot she was "*that* woman from Boston*" and thought of her as their own. In 1911 she wrote to her sister Anna:

". . . the unexpected has happened. I found among my letters one from President Luther of Trinity saying, 'I am exceedingly pleased that I am able to notify you that at their meeting, held on April 29th, the Trustees of Trinity College voted to confer upon you the degree of Master of Arts Honoris Causa, in recognition of your distinguished services to the City and your position as an educator, for that is what you are. I sincerely hope that you will accept, and that on Commencement Day, June 28th, I shall have the pleasure of handing you your diploma.'

"I accepted. . . . What made Trinity do it I can't imagine, and don't know whether there are other women to be honored."

There were no other women, and she was the first. "Hail, first Daughter of Trinity!" President Luther said, when making the presentation, and a newspaper account of the occasion comments, "so long was the applause the course of presentation was interrupted."

In 1925, the fiftieth anniversary of Miss Hewins' service as librarian in Hartford, Connecticut librarians and other friends, wishing to show their appreciation of her work, presented her with a sum of money. "They asked me to choose," she told Miss Moore, "between a trip to Europe and making it possible for the right kind of a girl to become a children's librarian."

"I hope," said Miss Moore, "that you chose Europe, that you are going everywhere you've never been and have always wanted to go in the most comfortable way possible. I hope you chose a big bag of gold pieces to spend freely."

She smiled and shook her head. "No, I didn't choose Europe. I can always get there somehow when I feel I must. A scholarship will last longer and it will be such fun to find the right girls for it."

Miss Hewins did not live long enough to choose the girls for the scholarship. In the summer of 1926 she went abroad at her own expense and in the fall to New York for Hallowe'en and to see the first copy of her *Mid-Century Child.* As usual she was interested in everything — the theater, the new art exhibits, the big five-and-ten-cent store on Fifth Avenue.

Four days after she came back to Hartford she died of pneumonia. Her funeral was held in the Center Church and although the family had stipulated " no flowers," they were there in abundance. " Two generations of Hartford people have benefited by coming in contact with Miss Hewins in their early years," said the minister at the funeral. " We give thanks for a half century of service. Let the city cherish the gift."

More than the city of Hartford " cherish the gift " Miss Hewins gave. In a telegram sent on the day of the funeral, Miss Louise Latimer of Washington, D. C., then chairman of the Children's Librarians' Section of the American Library Association, wrote: " Library work with children has lost its first friend and one of its best in the death of Miss Hewins. She generously stimulated, inspired and aided those working with children. Children's librarians will long keep her in happy memory."

The Caroline M. Hewins Scholarship and the Lectureship are worthy memorials; but a greater memorial is the firm foundation on which our library work with children is built, and for that foundation she was largely responsible.

This book is set in Electra, with Bodoni Book and Sylvan used for display, and is printed by the Thomas Todd Company of Boston. The paper is Kilmory Text made by W. C. Hamilton & Sons. The book was bound by the Stanhope Bindery, Boston.